ISBN: 978-0-9894338-9-1

Cover and Design: Jenna Stanbrough

On the cover:

The 1959 men's cross country team defended their NAIA National Cross Country Championship title. Members of the team pictured are from left to right: Lynn Reed, Gonzalo Javier, David Ohlde, Warner Wirta, Dennis Matheson, Paul Whiteley.

This picture hung for many years in the ESU Health, Physical Education, Recreation and Athletic building. As an athlete, a coach and a faculty member, I walked by it hundreds of times. It is my favorite picture that represents ESU cross country. – *M.S.*

Roho Publishing

4040 Graphic Arts Rd

Emporia, KS 66801

www.rohopublishing.com

Steve Hawkins originally wrote *A History of the Track/Field and Cross Country Teams at Emporia State University, 1900-1984* as his master's thesis. Over the last thirty years, ESU teams have continued to add to the legendary tradition. Mark Stanbrough added the years from 1984-2015 and edited the original Hawkins thesis to fit into a book format. Pictures have been added to help tell the historical story.

About Roho Publishing

When Kip Keino defeated Jim Ryun in the 1968 Olympic Games at 1500 meters he credited the win to "Roho." Roho is the Swahili word for spirit demonstrated through extraordinary strength and courage. The type of courage and strength that can be summoned up from deep within that will allow you to meet your goals and overcome the challenges in life. Roho Publishing focuses on the spirit of sport and is designed to inspire, encourage, motivate and teach valuable life lessons.

Dedication

I would like to thank my daughter, Jenna Stanbrough for being my right hand person. She has been an integral part in editing, designing and creating the final product of this book.

A special thanks goes to my family. My mom and dad supported me in my desire to be an athlete. My wife, Wendy has encouraged me throughout my career. My three daughters, whom I was fortunate enough to coach all three in cross country and track, are lifetime cross country and track and field fans.

I would like to thank all the coaches and fellow teammates I have had over the years who made a difference in my life. I would also like to thank the athletes whom I have had the privilege to coach over the years. Each of these individuals have taught me much about the qualities to be successful in life – good character, integrity, a strong work ethic, dedication and perseverance.

Mark Stanbrough

I would like to thank Dr. Patricia McSwegin, Dr. Bill Tidwell, Dr. Richard Keller and Dr. Fred Markowitz for their help and guidance with this project.

A special thanks goes to Coach Tidwell, who inspired the project and for whom it is written.

Thanks also to Mom, Dad and John for their assistance with the project.

Steve Hawkins

Acknowledgements

Special thanks go to Kylie Lewis from ESU Archives for her help in retrieving much needed information and the archives for allowing us to use the information in the book. Thanks to ESU Media and Marketing for the courtesy use of photos and information. The ESU athletic department, particularly Don Weast, Steve Blocker and Eric Wellman provided valuable help in finding results.

The History of Emporia State Cross Country: A Legendary Tradition of Distance Running

Table of Contents

Preface

I came to Emporia State in the fall of 1974 full of excitement to be a college student-athlete. I loaded up my 1969 Chevrolet Impala and drove the 100 miles from the small town of Mound City, Kansas to the big city of Emporia. As a graduate in the first class of Jayhawk-Linn High School in 1973, my high school had only offered football, basketball and track, and I enjoyed playing all three. When I came to ESU, I had never ran cross country. In fact, I had never seen a cross country race and had no idea how far you had to run. After meeting with Coach Philip Delavan in the summer of 1974, he recommended I run cross country. His famous words of, "It will make you a better 800 runner" eventually became prophetic. However, when I arrived at ESU, I had no idea what I was about to get into. Within a couple of weeks I went from my 25 miles a week training to 100 miles a week. It's a miracle my body survived! My first year was a challenge to say the least, but as the body and mind adapted, I did improve every year as a cross country runner.

My main event in track and field was the 800 meters and Coach Delavan was right. In a supporting ESU environment, I improved to compete at the national level. As I reflect back on my experiences as an athlete, I don't remember every race; however, my strongest memories are of the people that I was able to associate with on a daily basis- my teammates. It was during my running days at ESU that I began to learn of the legendary ESU cross country/track and field history. Bill Tidwell was the athletic director and I knew he held the school 800 record. I heard people talk about world-class shot putter Al Feuerbach and I was fortunate to be a teammate with Kathy Devine, the collegiate record holder in the shot put. However, my knowledge of ESU track and cross country history was very limited.

In 1984, a mere 10 years after a naïve student-athlete began attending ESU, I became the head cross country and track and field coach at ESU. It was during those eight years as the head coach that I began to deeply appreciate the magnificent history of the legendary ESU program.

After coaching at ESU, I remained teaching at ESU, in various roles of professor, department chair and director of coaching education. I have remained in close contact with ESU coaches and athletes and the sports of track and field and cross country as a high school coach and official. My appreciation of and respect for the ESU legends has continued to grow. When I share the stories with current athletes, most have little knowledge of the athletes that came before them. I believe it is important to tell the stories. The stories of legendary ESU athletes are motivating, energizing and create a tremendous sense of pride. I am a Hornet and I am proud to have ran, coached and have been associated with ESU for over forty years.

This book is dedicated to the many athletes and coaches who have established the proud, legendary tradition of cross country and track and field and at Emporia State University.

-Coach Mark Stanbrough, B.S.E. 1977, M.S. 1979

Preface

In the spring of 1984, I sat with my coach, advisor and mentor, Dr. Bill Tidwell, to discuss ideas for my master's thesis. He casually proposed the idea of writing about the history of track & field at ESU. Although my major was Physical Education, I was intrigued. The ESU Athletics Hall of Fame was in its infancy, and I'd seen several impressive track & field alumni inducted, including Coach Tidwell, so I took on the challenge. As I reached into the history of the program, I was drawn in more than I ever imagined that I could be. Hour upon hour was spent viewing microfiche in William Allen White Library, and the more that I discovered, the more that I wanted to know. I could not believe how incredible the history of the program was. Luck was on my side as well; one day a baseball coach approached me and asked did I want the track junk they had found in Welch Stadium. I assumed it was old equipment, but I said yes all the same. There was indeed old equipment, but there was also a binder that contained track & field results dating from the 1920's up through the 1960's. It turned out Coach Welch had been a meticulous record keeper. These records allowed me to confirm results gleaned from stories in the Gazette, yearbooks and other sources, as well as to establish top 10 performer lists for all events. Letters sent to alumni brought a response rate far greater than I ever expected, and provided amazing and amusing stories to include in the document. I still recall the sense of relief and disappointment that I felt when I sent the paper to the binder. I was relieved that the project was complete, as I had worked harder on that project than perhaps any other before or since. However, it was tinged with disappointment, as I didn't believe that I had completely encapsulated the history of the program, and I knew that the history was not going to stop with 1984. I'm very pleased that Mark continued to record the history of the ESU track and cross country programs, and is bringing this book to life. I'm also very proud to be a part of the ESU track and cross country heritage.

-Steve Hawkins, B.S.E. 1983, M.S. 1985

Foreword

I started coaching at Iowa State University and I always had a great respect for Fran Welch and the Emporia State program. After Iowa State, I went to the University of Central Missouri as the head track and field coach. Fran Welch called one day and asked if I would be interested in the track job at Emporia and I said, "you bet." He asked me not to tell anyone that I had the job. Fran hand-picked me as the coach.

Emporia State was one of the greatest jobs in the world. I loved being in Emporia and clearly loved coaching there and working with All-American and world record holders. After Emporia State I went to the University of Texas and retired but came out of retirement to coach at Round Rock High School. I told the Round Rock High athletes stories of the great athletes at Emporia State like Al Feuerbach and it helped them to work harder as they were inspired by the stories.

Emporia State was a very important part of my coaching career. Emporia State will always be a special place that is near and dear to my heart where Mary Jane and I spent some of the best years of our lives.

-Coach Phil Delavan

The reader of this book will be presented with the comprehensive history of the track and field/cross country program at Kansas State Normal School, Kansas State Teachers College and currently Emporia State University. The rich heritage of track and field at ESU was made possible by several outstanding state, national and internationally known coaches. These coaches have been successful working with modest facilities and budget.

As Fran Welch once said, "give me a talented athlete and he/she will make me a good coach." One may wonder why so many talented athletes choose to attend ESU. I believe for two reasons; first the personalities, knowledge, and skills of the coaches and second; ESU has always had the philosophy of promoting the academic program as well as the athletic program. My experience and observation has been that student-athlete programs motivate students to do the very best they can in the classroom and in athletics. Strong student-athlete programs provide the student with knowledge, skills and awareness to be successful in life.

ESU will continue to attract talented new students by providing high quality student athletics "for the common good."

-Coach Bill Tidwell

When I came to ESU in August of 1992, the university was in a transition period. We were moving into NCAA DII and full membership in MIAA. It was not hard for me to adjust, as I had been in the NCAA at the University of Nebraska the previous 7 years. But I got the feeling in talking to the coaches that they were really used to NAIA and their history had been that for so long that they and the programs were going to have to adjust. I also had run at the MIAA level at Northeast Missouri State University (Truman). I knew it was a great DII Conference to belong to.

In the fall of 1992, I took on the challenge of heading up the Cross Country and Track and Field program with a facility that was on its last days. That first year was the worst year I have ever had to train athletes and in fact ran many workouts on a cinder track down at the junior high athletic fields by Peter Pan Park. I also moved the cross country course from around the campus fields to Jones Park in Emporia where we began to paint a line around it every two weeks for workouts and our one home meet. This park was a vital part of my hill training for sprinters, jumpers and middle distance/distance runners.

We had a small team of less than 40 athletes both men and women. and very few new freshmen and two graduate assistant coaches in Will Waubaunsee and Don Farmer. Jonathon Oshel walked into my office that year and became an All American Javelin thrower. Between the facilities, budget and adjustments with athletes I almost felt I had made a mistake taking up Dr. Quayle's decision to hire me. At Nebraska our phone budget was larger than the operations budget at ESU for CC/T&F. I remember my wife Kathy and I having many talks that first semester and especially with her help saying to me "you wanted to be the head of your own program" and telling me she knew I could do this, we went about making the best of the situation and we said let's commit to making Emporia State our program. With that we took ownership in every part of the program for 19 years.

Recruiting was just going to work and reaching out to Kansas High schools – getting in the car and going out to schools and homes. Dr. Quayle gave me a university car with lots of miles on it and I proceeded to put many more on it and in fact ran if off the road in a flood coming back to Emporia about one o'clock in the morning one night. Two men recruits in that first class Troy Derley and Jason Stuke bought into my idea of the new track coming and wanted to be a part of building a solid DII program. I knew in visiting in their homes and with their parents they were the kind of young men and leaders that I needed. At the time I could not have understood the effect of them coming on the small amounts of scholarship aid I offered to what we began to accomplish in the years to come. They were certainly the cornerstone of getting the respect our program gained the first day they stepped on campus.

There are so many athletes over the 19 years to mention, but without these student athletes laying a foundation and the respect they brought to the program many of the others who came later would not have been possible. I am forever indebted to them for helping me build ESU to one of the most respected DII programs in the nation.

-Coach David Harris

Emporia State University cross country and track & field have been a huge part of my life for over a decade. When I came to ESU to compete as a distance runner in 2003, not only was I not aware of the legendary history of the program, I knew very little about running in general. Coming from a very small high school in Northeast Kansas, my training consisted of running two miles a day and competing in every distance race at track meets. With Dave Harris as my coach, I quickly fell in love with distance running and the ESU program. I decided at the end of my freshman year that I wanted to be a collegiate track and cross country coach. The experiences of hitting huge PRs, winning races, and traveling to great cities to compete are great memories but are a distant second to the relationships I developed with my coaches and teammates. Now that I have the opportunity to coach at my alma mater, it has become obvious that the greatest resource the ESU program has is its people. We may not have the same level of scholarship money or elaborate facilities as many of our rival universities, but the character and work ethic of our athletes allows them to be successful and carry on the great tradition of ESU cross country and track & field.

-Coach Eric Wellman

Men's Cross Country

Introduction

Cross country began in England in the early 1800s. The original races were run on much rougher terrain than today's courses. Participants back then had to run through streams, jump fences, and go through hedges. One of the earlier versions of cross country, called "paper chase," saw one group of runners leave first. This group would leave a paper trail for the second group to follow. The hares chased the hounds so to speak. Another early version, called "foot grind," had the competitors race from one point to the next but had no fixed route to follow. Participants could choose to cut through streams and jump over fences instead of going around them.

Towards the late 1800s, the competitions changed more toward today's style of race. The course was a fixed route, usually two miles or longer on trails, dirt, or grass. The sport became so popular in England, that in 1876, the English National Cross Country Championship took place. In 1878, the sport was introduced into the United States by William C. Vosburgh. At first, the sport served mainly as training for summer track and field athletics and many U. S. track and field athletes ran cross county to improve their stamina. It did not take long for the universities in the United States to pick up the sport, and nine years later, cross country running became a formal sport in the United States. Harvard was the first university to field a cross country team and many other universities followed. Despite the international popularity of cross country, the sport was dropped from the Olympics after 1924 due to it being an inappropriate summer sport. In the 1960s, the International Amateur Athletic Federation, which regulates cross country running, allowed women to run for the first time. The NCAA National Championship Races for the men began in 1938. The women began competing in the AIAW national championships in 1974, with the first NCAA Women's National Championship occurring in 1981.

1923

Due to the great success being experienced by the Kansas State Normal School (KSN) program, trackmen began working out early during the fall of 1923. About 25 of the new men were enrolled in a track class, taught by Bob Dunning that met three days a week. A cross country team was formed for the first time since the war, and the harriers raced against Fairmount College, losing 28-56. Since the early days of the program, cross country running had served as a means of fall training for trackmen. For a few years prior to the World War I war and continuing after 1923, the Yellowjackets' cross country team competed against other schools. Nevertheless, it was not considered an intercollegiate sport and was still basically a fall training program.

1924 Track and Field Team: Cross Country Training
A cross country team was formed and raced against Fairmount College.

1946

During the boom years that followed World War II, the competitive sport of cross country re-entered the picture at Kansas State Teacher's College. For the first time in years, Emporia State competed in cross country meets during the fall of 1946. Eighteen men tried out for the team, three of whom had been outstanding high school performers. Tom Carr, who had competed for the 1946 Hornet track team, had been the state high school 880-yard champ in 1942, and Dwight Waddell won the 880 at the Kansas State high school meet in 1946. Bob Karnes was the most outstanding, however. Karnes had won the Kansas State high school mile in 1942 and 1943, and he was also the Missouri Valley Amateur Athletic Federation (MVAAU) mile champ in 1943.

The team demonstrated their running prowess at the 1946 homecoming game with a 2 mile run on the track at halftime of the football game. Karnes came through the mile at 5:00 and finished in 1st in 10:32.6. Gale Stacey followed in 2nd and Charles Moore was 3rd.

Karnes was the Hornets' top finisher in the 1946 National Intercollegiate Cross Country meet held in Des Moines, Iowa, taking 8th out of a field of 56 runners. His high finish helped lead E-State to a 5th place team finish, behind Drake, Notre Dame, Michigan and Milwaukee College. Other runners for the Hornets were Waddell in 24th, Carr in 35th, Stacy in 37th and Kenneth Schwartz in 39th. When the 1947 track season opened, Karnes was gone, having transferred to KU. Karnes went on to an outstanding career with the Jayhawks. He was the Big 6 indoor two-mile champ in 1947-48-49, the Big 6 outdoor two-mile champ in 1947-48-49, and the Big 6 outdoor mile champ in 1948-49-50. Karnes also served as KUs captain in 1949 and 1950.

1947-1953

No record has been found of KSTC competing in cross country during the years 1947-1953. Cross country returned at KSTC in the fall of 1954.

1954

Bill Tidwell returned from the military just in time to lead the cross country team fielded by KSTC at the intercollegiate level. Tidwell had won the 1951 2-mile and mile runs at the 1951 CIC track meet before his military duty. During his military years he won the All-Armed Services Track and Field Championships 880 in 1:51.0, beating Wes Santee. Dr. William Schnitzer was coach for the Hornet harriers because Welch was busy with his head football duties. The Hornets competed in three dual meets and two triangular meets with a very young team, and Tidwell led Emporia by winning every meet except the Oklahoma A & M tri, where he finished behind A & M's three Norwegian runners. At Drake, Tidwell captured the 3-mile in 15:00 followed by Ray Velasquez in 5th and Francis Gangel in 7th. ESU defeated Pittsburg State in a dual held at the Emporia Country Club

William Schnitzer: First ESU Cross Country Coach

Schnitzer served one year as the Hornet coach in 1954 before Fran Welch assumed the position in 1955.

which the runners considered a tough course. Tidwell captured first over the 4-mile course in 21:58, followed by Velasquez in 2nd, as the Hornets beat Oklahoma Baptist.

Tidwell was the only Hornet to compete in the NCAA meet in East Lansing, Michigan, as freshmen were not allowed to compete at the NCAA national meet. Tidwell was a sophomore and the remainder of the team was freshmen. Tidwell finished 6th in the field of 117 runners to earn All-American recognition. Al Frame of Kansas University won in 19:54, and Tidwell finished in 20:12, which was his best 4-mile time of the year.

1955

Fran Welch was the Hornets' cross country coach in the fall of 1955, having given up the head football coaching duties to Keith Caywood. Welch inherited a young team, but one that was again led by Tidwell.

Tidwell won five of the seven meets he competed in, including a win over Al Frame of Kansas, the defending NCAA individual champ, in the Midwest AAU open in Iowa. Tidwell's only regular season loss was by .4 seconds to Sture Landquist of Oklahoma A & M, and Tidwell ended the season with a 10th place finish in the NCAA meet. Because of the rule against freshmen entries in the NCAA meet, Welch did not believe KSTC could field a representative team, so Tidwell was the only Hornet entry.

Francis Welch: Coach
Francis G. "Fran" Welch was chosen to succeed Bill Hargiss as head football and track coach. Welch came to KSTC in 1914 as an undergraduate, and earned letters in football, basketball and baseball. After a stint in the service during the World War, Welch attended Kansas State as a graduate student. In 1922, after coaching at Roosevelt High School for two years, Welch became a full-time coach and teacher at KSTC. Welch assisted Hargiss in football and track from 1922 to 1928. Welch continued to coach football through the 1954 season and then gave up the head football position to become the head cross country coach.

1956

Two new events were on the 1956 cross country schedule, with the CIC and the NAIA adding cross country championship meets. Several quality runners joined with Tidwell to provide the Hornets with a strong team, and the only loss KSTC suffered during the regular season was to Oklahoma A & M. Included in the victories was a quadrangular win over K-State, Wichita and Drake, and the CIC championship. Emporia was paced by Bill Tidwell's seventh straight cross country victory in winning the first Central Conference meet. The harriers scored 19 points, winning five of the first six places. The meet was held over a 4-mile course that stretched from the Emporia State Stadium around the Emporia Country Club and back. Tidwell clocked 20:27, Dunn was 3rd in 21:33, Velasquez 4th in 21:38, Lawrence Jones, 5th in 21:45, and Francis Gangel 6th in 21:47.

However, the Hornet team finished a disappointing 4th in the NAIA meet, with South Dakota State taking the title, while CIC rival Fort Hays placed 2nd. Tidwell went unbeaten during the regular season, setting four course records in seven races. However, Tidwell was upset in the NAIA meet on a course that was

covered by six inches of snow. Ray Manion of University of Redlands (California) kicked past him in the last 30 yards. Artie Dunn, along with Tidwell, earned All-America honors by placing 9th. Lawrence Jones was 23rd, Ray Velasquez 31st, and Francis Gangel 34th.

Artie Dunn: All-American
Artie Dunn became the second cross country All-American in ESU history when he finished 9th at the 1956 NAIA National Cross country Championships.

1957

The 1957 Hornet cross country team did not have an outstanding individual to lead them as Tidwell had done for three years, but a strong nucleus of runners helped KSTC remain on top of the CIC. Gonzalo Javier, Warner Wirta, Fran Gangel, Ray Velasquez and Dennis Matheson placed 2-3-4-6-8 respectively in the conference to lead E-State to the crown. Another strong grouping helped the Hornets to a 5th place finish in the NAIA nationals, where Velasquez was the top finisher in 22nd, closely followed by Wirta in 23rd, Gangel in 24th, Matheson in 26th, and Javier in 39th. The season had not been outstanding in terms of wins and losses, but this was mainly due to competition against larger schools.

1958

The Hornet harriers returned a strong nucleus of runners in the fall of 1958, including Paul Whiteley, Dennis Matheson, Warner Wirta, and Gonzalo Javier, and these men led KSTC to the most successful season since the inception of the sport at E-State. Except for a 7th place finish at the NCAA small college meet, the Hornets went unbeaten during the season. Whiteley won the NCAA small college meet over a 4-mile course in 20:43, finishing 20 yards clear of the field. The Hornets had four of the top finishers in the 13-team field but their fifth man finished 92nd to swell their point total. David Ohlde was a freshman on the team, but he was not eligible to compete in the meet because of the NCAA rule barring freshmen. Wirta finished 12th, Matheson, 24th, Javier 35, and Stephen Counts 92nd.

Bill Tidwell: All-American
Bill Tidwell, known more for his track and field exploits, was also an outstanding cross country runner. He earned three All-American honors, placing 6th in the NCAA Nationals in 1954, 10th in the NCAA Nationals in 1955 and 2nd in the inaugural 1956 NAIA National Championships.

Included in the victories was a third straight CIC title and the NAIA National Championship. This was the first national championship ever won by a KSTC athletic team.

Whiteley led the Hornet harriers through the season, winning every regular season meet. He ended the season placing 1st in the NCAA college meet and 3rd in the NAIA meet. Also earning All-America honors at the NAIA meet were Matheson, who finished one second behind Whiteley in 4th, and Wirta, who placed 11th. David Ohlde, Javier, and Lynn Reed rounded out the national championship team.

1959

The Hornet harriers opened the 1959 season with outstanding prospects, returning the entire 1958 NAIA national championship team intact. These men carried E-State through the regular season with only one blemish on the record, a 2nd place finish to Howard Payne College, Texas, in its own invitational. Paul Whiteley again paced the Hornets through the season, winning seven of the eight races he ran, including a successful defense of his NCAA college division title to lead KSTC to a 2nd place team finish behind South Dakota State. The Hornet harriers turned in a strong performance to defend their CIC title with Whiteley, Wirta, Matheson, Javier, and Ohlde taking the first five places to record a perfect score for KSTC. Whiteley posted the winning time of 20:14 for the 4-mile course. E-State ended the very successful season claiming their second consecutive NAIA title, defeating Kearney State, Nebraska, by four points. Whiteley, in his last appearance for the Hornets, finished 2nd in the race in 21:21 to earn All-American honors along with teammates Wirta, who finished 5th, and Matheson, who finished 11th. Ohlde, Reed, Javier, and freshman Peter Clarke rounded out the national championship squad.

Warner Wirta: All-American

Warner Wirta was a vital part of two national championship teams while running for KSTC. Wirtha placed 11th in the 1958 national meet and improved to 5th in the 1959 national meet.

NAIA National Champions: 1959

The 1959 men's cross country team defended their national title, defeating Kearney State by four points. Paul Whiteley finished 2nd, followed by fellow All-Americans Warner Wirta and Dennis Matheson. They recorded a perfect score at the CIC conference meet.

1960

The 1960 Hornet cross country team fell off quite a bit from the previous two years as three of the members of the national championship teams of 1958 and 1959 were gone, and a fourth ran in only one meet. Senior Dennis Matheson came on strong at the end of the year to lead the Hornets to their fifth straight CIC title, which KSTC won easily. Matheson won in 21:36, followed by John Evely in 2nd, Richard Woelk in 3rd, Lynn Reed in 5th, and Dick Clasen in 7th. E-State harriers finished 8th in the NAIA meet, paced by Matheson's 12th place finish, which earned him All-American honors for the third straight year.

1961

The 1961 Hornet cross country squad was an unknown entity at the start of the season. The top returnees were sophomore Richard Woelk and senior David Ohlde, the latter a member of the 1958 and 1959 national championship teams who had missed most of the 1960 season. Welch had to depend on freshmen to fill out the squad, and he had an outstanding group of them, led by John Camien (from Sewenhaka High School in New York), Andy Prescia, and Clarence Herpich. This team provided Welch with some pleasant surprises. Emporia State totaled 25 points to win its sixth consecutive CIC cross country championship at the snow-filled Emporia Airport course. John Camien won the individual title by

Dennis Matheson: All-American

Dennis Matheson finished 4th in the 1958 NAIA National Cross Country Championships to help lead ESU to their first national title. The next year, Matheson finished 11th in helping the Hornets win their second consecutive national championship. Matheson became a three-time All-American by placing 12th in 1960.

edging Bob Mohler of Fort Hays at the finish line, finishing the 4-mile course in 21:40, a mere second ahead of Mohler, who led for most of the race. Woelk and Prescia were 3rd and 4th, with Charles Atkins, 8th, Herpich 9th, Reed 11th, and Ohlde 12th.

The Hornets nosed conference rival Fort Hays 73-75 to win a third NAIA National Championship. Camien and Woelk led the young Hornets through the season, alternating as top runner. Woelk and Camien finished 6th (21:38) and 12th (22:08), respectively, in the NAIA meet to both earn All-American honors. Rounding out the national championship squad were Herpich in 20th, Lynn Reed in 21st, and Ohlde in 28th. Charles Atkins, and Prescia completed the team. The top five Hornets finished only one minute and 10 seconds apart over the 4-mile national course to take the title.

1962

The Hornets added an outstanding runner in 1961 that would add to their already established distance legacy. Ireland Sloan had transferred to KSTC in the spring of 1961 from Morehead State, Kentucky. He had never run competitively before enrolling at Morehead in the fall of 1960, but was so outstanding that Dr. Nolan Fowler, the coach at Morehead, suggested that Sloan transfer to a larger school. Fowler recommended Houston, Oregon, and KSTC, and Sloan chose Emporia State because of the size of the school. Sloan was not the first outstanding runner sent to Emporia by Dr. Fowler, as he had also sent Paul Whiteley a few years earlier. Sloan ran unattached in meets during the 1961 spring and fall seasons, turning in some outstanding performances, the best of which was a 6th place finish overall and the second American in the National AAU 10,000-meter during the 1961 summer. Sloan and Camien combined over the next several seasons to form one of the most potent distance duos in the history of the NAIA.

Ireland Sloan: National Champion
Ireland Sloan transferred from Morehead State Kentucky in 1961 and had an illustrious career with the Hornets. He won the NAIA national championship in cross country in 1962 and earned three cross country All-American honors.

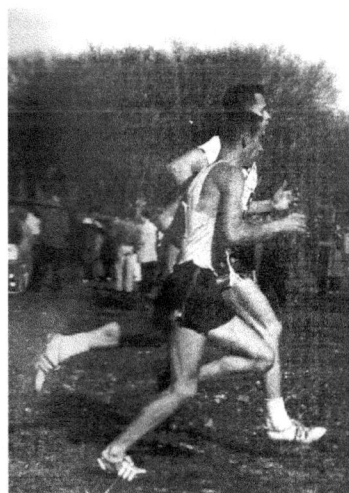

Prior to the 1962 cross country season, Coach Welch had the following to say about his team:

> "I think we have the best squad that we have ever had. Our squad last year had depth, but a mediocre top. This year we have depth, but we also have extremely good leading men." (KSTC Bulletin, Vol. 62, No. 3, p. 4)

The previous year's squad Welch referred to had been CIC and NAIA champions, pointing towards an extremely successful season.

The 1962 Hornet harriers lived up to Welch's expectations, winning four of six regular season meets with the only losses coming at the hands of NCAA schools in the University of Denver Invitational and the University of Texas Invitational. The Hornets ended the season repeating as CIC and NAIA champions, and finished 3rd in the NCAA small college meet. Individually, Sloan and Camien were outstanding, finishing 1-2, respectively, in four meets and 1-3, respectively, in two other meets.

The Hornets won their seventh consecutive CIC title edging out Fort Hays by the score of 26-30. Sloan set a new CIC meet record over the Emporia Country Club golf course covering four miles in 20:11. Camien followed Sloan in second with Woelk in 4th, and Herpich in 8th.

Sloan turned in the most notable performances, posting the nation's fastest 3-mile and 4-mile cross country times of 14:23 and 19:20, respectively. He was also the CIC and NAIA champion, setting an NAIA record of 20:22 for the four-mile distance. Camien, Woelk and Clarence Herpich placed 3rd, 7th, and 13th, respectively, in the NAIA meet to also earn All-American recognition as the Hornets beat Fort Hays State 50-95 to capture their fourth NAIA national title in five years. Rounding out the championship squad were Jim McCann (40th), Chuck Atkins (66th) and Peter Clarke (82nd). Camien led the Hornets in the NCAA small college meet with a 2nd place finish, while Sloan finished two seconds behind in 3rd place. Woelk was 9th and Herpich was 15th. KSTC's regular fifth runner, McCann, was unable to compete in the NCAA meet because of the rule against freshmen, and 90 men placed between fourth man Herpich and fifth man Atkins to wreck the Hornets' chances to win the title as they finished 3rd.

Richard Woelk: All-American
Richard Woelk led a young Hornet team throughout the season and finished 6th at the 1962 NAIA National Championships to earn All-American honors. Woelk's efforts led to a team national championship.

Clarence Herpich: All-American
Clarence Herpich placed 13th in the 1962 national cross country meet as the Hornets won their fourth national championship in five years.

NAIA National Champions: 1962
The 1962 Hornets won the CIC and NAIA national meets defeating Fort Hays State. Ireland Sloan and John Camien led the way with a 1-2 finish. The Hornets dominated the NAIA national competition winning four national championships in five years.

With the top five runners from the 1962 NAIA cross country championship team returning in 1963, KSTC again fielded a powerful team. Camien, Sloan, Woelk and Herpich were all among the top runners in the NAIA. The combination of Camien and Sloan was again a potent duo, with Camien leading the way throughout the season. The pair took 1st and 2nd in eight of the 10 meets KSTC competed in, and in the remaining two, one or the other did not compete. Camien had a very successful season, winning nine times in 10 starts, including the State Federation, the CIC, the NCAA College and the NAIA titles, setting four course records. His only defeat was at the hands of Vic Zwolak of Villanova in the NCAA Championships. Sloan finished as runner-up in the State Federation, the CIC, the NCAA College and the NAIA meet. However, he was unable to run in the NCAA Championships due to his status as a four-year athlete.

John Camien: National Champion
John Camien competed for the Hornets from 1961-1965. In cross country, he was a two time NAIA National Champion, winning in 1963 and 1964, and three-time conference winner. He also won the NCAA small college meet in 1963. In track he won 16 conference championships and five NAIA championships, including the 1500 meters four straight years.

Sloan and Camien

The Hornet team also had outstanding success as the harriers finished 2nd in the Federation meet behind KU and won the CIC meet, edging a strong Fort Hays team by three points by the score of 27-30. The CIC was held at the Emporia airport course and the Hornets made it eight straight CIC titles. Camien took the win in 19:23, followed by Sloan in 19:32. Woelk was 4th, Herpich 8th, McCann 13th, Finger 14th, and Myron Staskow 19th.

KSTC added yet another national title to its collection, winning the NCAA Small College meet held at the Chicago Golf Club by 130 points over an Akron University team with an Emporia team of Camien, Sloan, Woelk, Herpich, Robert Finger and Jim McCann. Camien took the individual title in 19:16, beating the old record by 43 seconds. Sloan was 2nd in 19:29, Woelk was 10th, Herpich was 17th, Finger 45th, and McCann 79th.

The season ended on a sour note, however. Despite the 1-2 finish by KSTC's two front-runners, Fort Hays upset the Hornets in the NAIA meet by the score of 53-69. Camien took the national title in 20:23, only one second off the record time set by Sloan the year before. Sloan finished 2nd in in 20:31.

Woelk earned All-American honors for the third consecutive year by placing 12th, and Herpich just missed making All-American status with an 18th place finish. Hays pulled off the upset by placing five men among the first 21 runners, while Finger, Emporia's fifth, placed back in 49th. The victory began a series of strong national finishes for Fort Hays Coach Alex Francis' Tigers as the championship team was composed of one just junior and six sophomores.

1964

In the fall of 1964, Camien and Herpich returned to give the Hornet cross country team two outstanding seniors. However, the team lacked the depth of the squads of the previous years and KSTC finished the season with only two team victories. The Hornets lost to Fort Hays four times during the regular season, so it came as no surprise when the Tigers ended Emporia State's eight-year reign in the CIC with a low score of 18 points compared to Emporia's 3rd place total of 77. The Hornet harriers finished 5th in the NAIA meet,

NCAA College Meet Champions: 1963
KSTC added yet another national title to its collection in 1963, winning the NCAA Small College meet by 130 points with the team of Camien, Sloan, Woelk, Herpich, Robert Finger, and Jim McCann.

while Hays fell to 3rd. For the first time in meet history, a non-Kansas college won, as Howard Payne of Texas dethroned the Fort Hays Tigers. With 20 teams represented and 144 runners the NAIA meet was the largest championship to date at the annual met held in Omaha, Nebraska.

Although the team success was not as noteworthy, John Camien continued his success, again going unbeaten throughout the season while repeating his victories in the State Federation meet, the CIC, and the NAIA. Camien became the first man to win two consecutive NAIA cross country titles. Despite a cold, stiff win, Camien finished only three seconds off the meet record set in 1962 by Ireland Sloan.

The Hornets' other senior, Herpich, just missed earning All-America recognition, finishing 16th in the NAIA meet. Included among the remainder of the Hornet squad was freshman Robert Camien, John's younger brother, who was to continue the Camien's success at KSTC after John's graduation.

For a while, the names of Yellowjacket and Hornet were used interchangeably. The evolution of the school mascot went from a stereotypical hornet to "Corky" the Hornet, who first appeared in 1934 by student Paul Edwards.

Fran Welch Era

The 1965 track season capped the long and successful coaching career of Francis G. Welch. Welch's accomplishments in his 38 years as head coach rank him as one of the most outstanding track coaches in the United States. His Emporia State teams claimed eight conference cross country crowns, six indoor track conference titles, 12 outdoor track conference crowns, four NAIA cross country championships, one NCAA small college cross country title, and one NAIA track and field title. In NAIA competition, Welch-coached athletes won 18 individual titles, more than any other school through 1965. Welch coached international teams that represented the United States abroad, including the 1960 Women's Olympic track team. He was honored in 1960 when the Emporia State stadium was renamed Welch Stadium, and he was a charter inductee into the NAIA Hall of Fame and the Emporia State Athletic Hall of Honor. His contributions to the Hornet cross country/track and field programs have been unmatched by anyone in the history of the university.

1965

Philip Delavan was chosen to succeed Coach Welch as head cross country and track coach in 1965.

Delavan inherited a very young cross country team in 1965, with Bob Finger the only returning senior on a squad loaded with 18 freshmen. The youth showed, as the Hornets picked up only three team victories and fell to 3rd in the CIC meet behind Hays and Pittsburg. Hays dominated the conference meet, taking six of the top seven places with Don Lukin of Fort Hays winning in 19:35 at Emporia's airport course. David Brinsko was the top ESU runner. Fort Hays' depth carried the Tigers to the NAIA title. Pittsburg finished 4th in

Philip Delavan: Coach

Philip Delavan became the ESU head track and field and cross country coach in 1965. He had served as head track coach at Central Missouri State University from 1963 to 1965, previous to which he had been an assistant at Baylor University for one year and an assistant at Iowa State University for two years. Delavan had attended school at Iowa State from 1955-1959, during which time he was one of the best shot putters in the nation. In 1957, he placed 1st in the shot put in the Kansas Relays, and placed 6th in the finals of the NCAA shot put that same year.

the national meet, while KSTC placed 12th, slipping out of the top 10 for the first time in the decade. The Hornets were led through the season by sophomore Bob Camien and freshman Brinsko, the latter coming to E-State as the New York state high school two-mile champion. Despite the lack of outstanding team

15

results, the youth of the team gave a strong outlook for the future. Also adding to the team results throughout the year were Simone, Bob Symanski, Clifford De Pass, John Grella, and John Swaim.

1966

The 1966 cross country season opened with a great deal of promise, as the Hornet harriers won the Wichita Invitational, defeating Fort Hays and Pittsburg, among others. Freshman Dennis Delmott was the Hornets' top finisher at Wichita, followed closely by junior Bob Camien, and these two alternated leading KSTC throughout the season. However, the Hornets' success against NAIA powers Hays and Pitt was short-lived. Emporia lost to Hays in the annual dual and finished 3rd behind the Tigers and Gorillas in the CIC.

Emporia was led in the CIC meet by Delmott who placed 4th in 21:39, followed by DePass, Bill Jacobs, Camien, Symanski, Roger Bruning and Jim Schnurr. The Hornets ended the season taking 13th place at the NAIA meet. Once again, the team Delavan fielded was very young, with the top six consisting of one junior, two sophomores and three freshmen. The team was hurt by the loss of David Brinsko to the service, who, as a freshman in 1965, had been one of the Hornets' top runners. At the NAIA meet, Delmott was the Hornets' top finisher in 33rd, Camien in 53rd, De Pass in 83rd, Jacobs in 89th, and Szymanski finished 121st to round out the scorers. Schnurr finished in 141st and Bruning in 169th.

1967

With the top seven runners back from 1966 and the return of David Brinsko from the service, the 1967 Hornet cross country team held a great deal of promise. They were very competitive, but unfortunately, hampering injuries and illness kept the Hornets from the results they had hoped for. E-State was at full strength only once during the season, when they scored a seven-point win over rival Fort Hays in a triangular meet. The powerful Tigers won the other four meetings between the two schools, including the CIC meet, where the Hornets finished 2nd. John Mason of Fort Hays State covered the tough 4-mile course in 20:03. E-State placed four men in the top 10 with Brinsko in 3rd in 20:33, Delmott in 5th in 20:57, Bob Symanski in 8th in 21:07, and Frank Zylor in 9th in 21:13. In both the CIC and NAIA meets, KSTC was handicapped by the illness of senior Bob Camien, who competed in both meets but was unable to finish as a top runner for the Hornets. Despite Camien's illness, the Emporia State harriers were able to finish 9th in the NAIA Championships. Zylor led the effort in 26th, Brinsko in 45th, Delmott in 67th, DePass in 81st, Camien in 97th and Jim Schnurr in 114th. Schnurr endured despite being spiked, losing his shoe and suffering a wound that took five stitches after the meet.

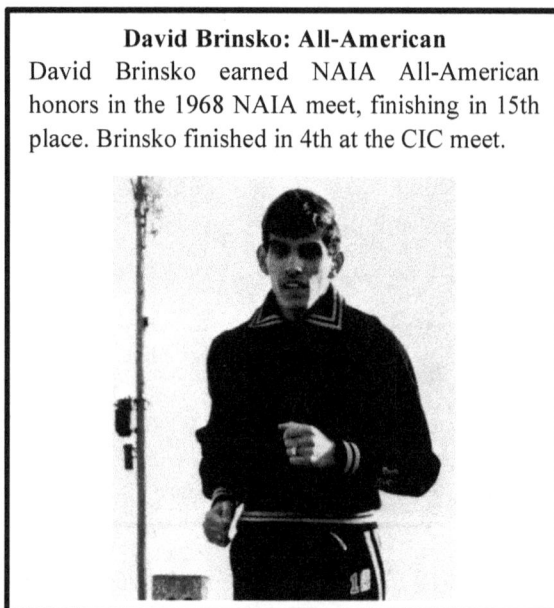

David Brinsko: All-American
David Brinsko earned NAIA All-American honors in the 1968 NAIA meet, finishing in 15th place. Brinsko finished in 4th at the CIC meet.

1968

The 1968 cross country season was the most successful in several years for the Hornets. KSTC boasted a very strong team with the return of Dennis Delmott, David Brinsko and Bob Szymanski, and the addition of outstanding freshmen Greg Carpenter, Dennis Nee, and Darrell Patterson. The Hornets opened the season with an upset victory over Fort Hays at the Wichita State Invitational, and came back two weeks later to whip the Tigers in a dual with a score of 24-35. This

---

An Olympic Ace

Fort Hays came up with an ace right before the 1968 CIC meet. Since the 1968 Olympics had been held in September, the NAIA had a special ruling allowing Olympic athletes to enroll in only one hour during the fall semester and still be eligible to compete. Fort Hays added Larbi Oukeda, a Moroccan Olympian, to their team in late October, and with Oukeda finishing 2nd behind teammate John Mason in the CIC, the Tiger's won the title over the Hornets by the score of 23-32. Oukeda also made the difference in the NAIA meet as Fort Hays nipped KSTC 106-110 to win the team title with Mason and Oukeda finishing 1st and 3rd, respectively. Without the Moroccan representing Hays, the Hornets would have won KSTC's fifth NAIA national cross country title.

---

early success left KSTC confident of gaining their first conference title since 1963. However, Fort Hays came up with an ace right before the CIC meet. Since the 1968 Olympics had been held in September, the NAIA had a special ruling allowing Olympic athletes to enroll in only one hour during the fall semester and still be eligible to compete.

Fort Hays took advantage of this rule to add Larbi Oukeda, a Moroccan Olympian, to their team in late October. With Oukeda finishing 2nd behind teammate John Mason in the CIC, the Tigers won the title over the Hornets by the score of 23-32. Without Oukeda in the race, Emporia State would have won the conference title 27-28. Delmott and Brinsko led the Hornets in the CIC with 3rd and 4th place finishes, respectively. Oukeda also made the difference in the NAIA meet as Fort Hays nipped KSTC 106-110 to win the 47 team meet with John Mason and Oukeda finishing 1st and 3rd, respectively. Delmott and Brinsko both earned All-American honors in the NAIA meet, finishing 12th and 15th, respectively. Delmott ran 24:33, with Brinsko in 24:46. Rounding out the national runner-up squad was Nee in 23rd, Szymanski in 30th, and Patterson in 36th, with Carpenter and Blaine Thomas finishing as sixth and seventh men.

1969

The 1969 cross country season opened with a great deal of promise, with the Hornets returning everyone from the national runner-up squad of 1968 except Bob Szymanski. KSTC was ranked 2nd in the NAIA behind rival Fort Hays for most of the season, and the Hornet harriers lost to the Tigers three times during the regular season. However, KSTC lived up to its high national ranking, as the only other teams that defeated the Hornets during the regular season were University of Texas at El Paso and KU at the OSU Invitational.

The Hornets placed five men in the top 10 and grabbed the team championship at the Missouri Valley Championships. The Hornets ran 2-3-5-7-10 to total 27 points and beat Fort Hays by 4 points. Delmott captured 2nd with a time of 24:50 over the 5-mile course. Other Hornet placers were Nee in 3rd, Brinsko in 5th, Patterson in 7th, and Blaine Thomas in 10th.

Unfortunately, the Hornets finished 3rd behind Fort Hays and Adams State, Colorado, in the first Rocky Mountain Athletic Conference championships, then finished a disappointing 6th in the NAIA meet to end the season on a sour note. Hays repeated as national champs and Adams State took 4th. Delmott capped a successful season by earning All-American honors for the second consecutive year, finishing in 9th place. His time for the wind-slowed 5-mile run was 25:12. The winning time was only 24:53, the slowest winning time in years. Nee placed 23rd, and Patterson 42nd. Damaging the Hornets' team chances, though, was E-State's other returning All-American, David Brinsko, finishing in 79th place. Blaine Thomas completed the ESU team in 91st.

Dennis Delmott: All-American
Dennis Delmott was a two-time All-American in cross country. Delmott earned All-American honors in the 1968 NAIA National Championships meet, finishing 12th and then repeated as an All-American in 1969 by finishing in 9th place.

1970

Coach Phil Delavan received a high honor when he was chosen as one of the coaches for the United States team in the World University Track and Field Games held in Turin, Italy. This was the first of many international coaching experiences Delavan enjoyed. He returned in September just in time for the cross country season, in what was definitely a rebuilding year. Dennis Nee, Darrell Patterson and Merv Harlan were the only returning lettermen, and these three led the Hornets through the season. The inexperienced Hornet harriers struggled early, but came on strong to finish a surprising 3rd in the RMAC meet behind Hays and Adams State, Colorado, and 2nd in the District 10 behind Hays despite Patterson missing the district with an injury. The Hornets earned these places on the strength of high finishes by Harlan and Nee, who placed 4th and 5th, respectively, in the RMAC, then reversed that order in taking 1st and 2nd in the district. The KSTC harriers ended the season placing 20th in the NAIA national meet, led by Harlan's 40th place finish.

1971

Youth was the dominant feature of the 1971 Hornet cross country team with two seniors, Dennis Nee and Darrell Patterson, leading a group of freshmen and sophomores. Because of inexperience-only two of the 19 were experienced, with six of the top 10 freshmen-the KSTC squad started the season slowly. The team steadily improved to finish the season with a 2nd place finish in the District 10 meet behind Hays while defeating Pittsburg for the first time during the season. The Hornets also tied for 1st with the powerful Tigers of Fort Hays in the MVAAU meet and finished 18th in the NAIA nationals. The Hornets placed only 5th in the RMAC, but this low finish was not indicative of the strength of the Hornet squad as evidenced by the fact that the teams that defeated KSTC in the meet-Adams State, Omaha, Fort Hays and Pittsburg-finished 1st, 9th, 10th and 19th, respectively, in the NAIA national meet.

In his senior year during the fall of 1971, Nee posted the most successful season by a Hornet harrier since the days of John Camien. Nee went unbeaten through the regular season with wins at Wichita, Emporia, Pittsburg, Southwest Missouri, and the MVAAU meets. He also won the conference title and ended the season with a 7th place finish in the NAIA national meet after being knocked down during the race.

Patterson, the other Hornet senior, turned in his best performance of the season, and one of the best of his cross country career, with a 3rd place finish at the RMAC meet. He ended the season placing 31st in the national meet despite coming in only 26 seconds behind Nee. Following for the Hornets were Rick Bishop in 65th, Tom Quammen in 162nd, Ray Van Sickle in 196th, Art Milliken in 204th, and Jim White in 221st. The Hornets finished 18th in the team standings with 450 points at the NAIA meet held at William Jewell College.

Dennis Nee: All-American
Dennis Nee was a track and cross country standout from 1968-1972. He earned All-American honors in cross country by finishing 7th at the 1971 national meet. He was 2nd in the 1972 NAIA national outdoor track meet in the 5,000. Nee was a member of the Australian World Cross Country Championship team in 1975.

1972

The loss of Nee and Patterson was difficult to replace in 1972, as only three lettermen returned. In an early season meet held at the Emporia Airport course, ESU finished 4th behind Marymount, Fort Hays, and Pittsburg State. The Hornets got used to running against Marymount and Hays, two of the top teams in the nation. Of the nine meets ESU ran, they faced Hays eight times and Marymount seven times. Brad Anderson led the Emporia effort, clocking 20:51 over the 4-mile course for 13th place. Rick Bishop led the Hornets at the Marymount Invitational, finishing 12th as the team finished 3rd in the three-team meet. Marymount's talented Irishman, Tony Brien, led his team to the District 10 title over the hilly 5-mile course, followed by Fort Hays and then ESU. Rick Bishop in 11th place led Emporia in 28:02, followed by Jim Hickey in 28:12, Brad Anderson in 28:12, Ray Van Sickle in 28:33, Anthony McRoberts in 28:49, Del Brandley in 28:51, and Art Milliken in 29:13.

Emporia wrapped up the 1972 season with a 4th place finish in the MVAAU meet. Brad Anderson took 13th in 25:36.

1973

Emporia State entered the 1973 season with a large number of freshmen challenging veterans for top spots. One of those freshmen, Steve Mosteller from Security, Colorado, won his first meet in 20:51 at the Southwestern Triangular to lead the Hornets to the title. Four different Hornets led throughout the race, including Art Milliken, who led until the last few yards when Mosteller passed him. Mosteller again led the Hornets at Wichita, placing 20th with a time of 21:04, as the team placed 5th.

ESU's home invitational had to find a different course when Highway 99, the road leading up to the home course at the airport, became flooded. The meet was run as a 4-mile road race near Camp Alexander east of town. Tony Brien of Marymount ran an outstanding time to win in 18:44. Fort Hays won the team title with ESU in 3rd. Del Brandley led ESU, finishing 12th in 20:52 and Greg Purkeypile emerged in 14th in 20:54.

Before the championship meets, ESU dueled Pittsburg and Fort Hays on consecutive weekends. In hosting the Gorillas, Pitt State went 1-2-3 and the Hornets took the next seven places. Unfortunately, that was not enough to beat Pitt. At Fort Hays, the Tigers won easily in taking the first four places. Leonard Hall led ESU in 5th in 28:09.

Four national berths were on the line at the District 10 meet. Pittsburg State won decisively on their home course and ESU finished 3rd to qualify for the national meet. Tony Brien of Marymount won by over a minute. E-State went 8-9-10 with Milliken (26:46), Chuck Weston (26:47), and Purkeypile (26:49). Bishop in 15th (27:00), Mosteller in 21st (26:26), Hall in 23rd (27:35), and Brandley in 29th (28:34) completed the team effort.

The Great Plains Athletic Conference meet was held after the District 10 meet and ESU took 4th behind the surprise winner, Northern Colorado. Milliken led ESU in 18th place in 26:34 and Purkeypile finished 20th.

The Hornets competed in the NAIA National Cross Country Championships and finished 22nd. Tony Brien of Marymount, whom the Hornets had gotten tired of seeing all year, won the NAIA national title, running a quick 23:42 over a 5-mile course.

1974

ESU won the Marymount Invitational when Greg Purkeypile finished 3rd in 26:10 behind the winning effort of Tony Brien of Marymount, the defending NAIA champion who won in 24:47, followed by Chuck Weston in 5th, Larry Grecian in 6th, and Leonard Hall in 7th. ESU dueled Fort Hays in a back and forth dual of great rivals, won by Fort Hays by a single point. The race for the individual title was exciting as the lead changed hands four times in the last mile of the 5-mile race, with the first three ESU runners posting personal best times. Hall placed 2nd in 25:34 with Purkeypile 3rd in 25:40. Grecian posted a 5th, Weston an 8th, and Milliken a 10th. A week later the Gorillas of Pittsburg State handed ESU a dual loss by a score of 19-38. ESU was led by Grecian and Purkeypile in 4th and 5th respectively. At the Missouri Valley AAU meet hosted by Emporia on a rainy day, ESU finished 3rd as a team behind Pittsburg State and Wichita State. Purkeypile led ESU in 8th with a 25:06 for the 5-mile course, with Hall also cracking the top 10 in 9th.

Emporia State finished 4th in the Great Plains Athletic Conference Cross Country Championships held at Pittsburg State. The Gorillas took the team title led by the winner Tyler Todd. The Hornets were led by Purkeypile, who finished 9th, Weston, who finished 18th, and Hall in 24th.

Emporia earned a national berth by placing 3rd at the District 10 race behind Pittsburg State and Fort Hays State. Purkeypile paced the Hornets by taking 8th in the field with a time of 26:02. Teammate Hall was just a few steps back, in 9th, in 26:05. Tony O'Brien, the defending national champion from Marymount, was the winner in 24:20.

At the national meet held in Salina, Kansas, the Hornets finished 26th out of the 53 competing schools. A scoring foul-up made the final results partially inaccurate. The trouble began when a runner fell down at the finish line and the finishers behind him were sent to a different finish chute. Milliken finished in a time of 26:21 and was placed 211th. However, Weston, and Hall, who ran behind Milliken in 26:26 and 26:27, were placed 136th and 137th. ESU lost an estimated two or three team places because of the foul-up. Even without the scoring difficulties, there was no doubt who won. Eastern New Mexico's Olympic medalist Mike Boit won in 23:45 and led his team to a low score of 28 points. Purkeypile led E-State in 54th place running 25:23. Mosteller was 226th in 27:06 and Brad Grooms was 236th in 27:13.

1975

On the strength of a group of juniors and sophomores who had gained a great deal of experience while struggling through the losing seasons, the 1975 Hornet cross country team regained the stature that had been missing during the previous three seasons. Again the Hornets did not post many team victories, winning only at the Marymount Invitational. However, this was because Fort Hays and Pittsburg had two of the best cross country teams in the NAIA, as was the case throughout most of the decade. Emporia Kansas State College had to run against one or both almost every week. Besides the victory at Marymount, the E-State harriers finished 3rd in both the conference and district meets behind Pitt and Hays, and ended the season with a 13th place finish in the NAIA nationals. Hays and Pitt placed 3rd and 8th, respectively, in the national meet. Junior Greg Purkeypile led the young Hornets through most of the season. He finished 4th and 5th, respectively, in the conference and district meets, and became EKSC's first cross country All-American since 1971 by taking 25th place in the NAIA meet

Greg Purkeypile: All-American

In 1975 and 1976, the top 25 finishers at the NAIA National Cross Country meet were awarded All-American status. Greg Purkeypile narrowly made the cut two consecutive years by placing 25th both years, earning the last All-American position.

with the 5-mile time of 25:38. Rick Tyler placed 98th, Leonard Hall 115th, Chuck Weston 58th, Jamie McPhee 168th, and Dave Ransom 287th. Top honors in the meet went to Kenya Olympic medalist Mike Boit in 24:23.

1976

The 1976 cross country season was extremely frustrating for the Hornet harriers who, despite being ranked in the top 15 in the NAIA throughout most of the season, were able to place only 3rd in the initial Central States Intercollegiate Conference championship meet and 4th in the NAIA District 10 meet, missing qualification for the nationals as a team. The reason for this frustration was that Pittsburg, Fort Hays, and Marymount had teams that also ranked among the best in the NAIA, and E-State finished behind the first two in the CSIC and behind all three in the district meet. Senior Greg Purkeypile again led the Hornets during the season, finishing as the top man for EKSC in every meet. He won the Marymount Invitational and led the Hornets to a 2nd place finish over a 10K course, losing to Fort Hays, but defeating a strong team in Marymount. Jamie McPhee in 7th (32:28), Robbie Harber in 13th (33:15), Mark Stanbrough in 17th (33:36), and John Burrows in 19th (33:40) completed the scoring.

Purkeypile placed 3rd individually in the district meet running 24:16, followed by McPhee in 12th (24:57) as both runners qualified for nationals. Harber (25:08), Burrows (25:35), Mike Mattox (26:03), Stanbrough (26:12), and Dave Ransom (26:20) completed the Hornet team at the district meet. Purkeypile repeated his finish from the 1975 national championship, placing 25th with the 5-mile time of 24:57 to earn All-American honors for the second consecutive year. Sophomore McPhee earned All-District 10 honors with a 12th place finish to also qualify for the NAIA meet as an individual, but he finished back in the pack against the national competition.

1977

The 1977 Hornet cross country team raced almost every week against Fort Hays and Pittsburg State, who were once again two of the top-ranked teams in the NAIA. The Hornets finished 2nd to Fort Hays in the Hays Invitational, the Marymount Invitational, and the Kansas Intercollegiate, 2nd to Pitt in a dual, and 3rd behind both at the Emporia Invitational.

In a quirk in the schedule, the Hornets had back-to-back meets on consecutive days. They finished 2nd in the five-team race at Fort Hays, led by Dave Ransom in 8th on a Friday and then came back the next day to post a perfect 15-50 score against Southwestern. The meet on the day prior served as a good warm-up as the Hornets posted fast times on the mostly flat 5-mile Southwestern course. The first seven Hornets across the line for the perfect score included Ransom in 24:36, Harber in 24:45, Chuck Grotto in 24:55, Tom Noonan in 24:59, Mike Maddox in 25:09, and Mark Stanbrough in 25:17.

The Hornets were 3rd in the CSIC meet hosted at the Emporia course at the airport. Fort Hays captured the title with Pittsburg 2nd, followed by ESU. Ransom led the charge in 11th in 25:59. A 3rd place finish in the district earned the Hornets a return trip to the NAIA national meet after a year's absence. Noonan finished as E-State's top man at the district meet, placing 13th to earn All-District honors. The Emporia State harriers placed 31st in the 59-team national field. Ransom led the national effort, followed by McPhee, Harber, Noonan, Grotto, Stanbrough, and Maddux.

Delavan Era

Phil Delavan, Emporia State's track and cross country coach since 1965, resigned in late August of 1978 to become the head women's track and cross country coach at the University of Texas. Delavan posted a very successful career as head of Emporia State's teams, coaching champions Richard Boehringer, Allen Feuerbach and Kathy Devine, as well as numerous All-Americans. Delavan had been widely recognized among his peers, having served as President of the NAIA Track Coaches Association and the NAIA Cross Country Coaches Association. He had also been selected a member of the high altitude training staff for the 1968 U.S. Olympic team, had served as a coach for the 1970 World University Games United States team and as manager for the 1973 World University Games U.S. team, and had served as field coach for the 1972 United States women's Olympic track team. Delavan coached 13 track and field All-Americans including three national champions as well as three cross country All-Americans in his tenure.

1978

Coach Dennis Delmott took over for the departed Phil Delavan and inherited a very strong Hornet cross country squad in 1978, with six returning lettermen and the addition of junior college transfer Greg Topham. E-State opened the season at the Wichita Invitational with very impressive results, placing 6th in a predominantly NCAA field while defeating defending NAIA champ Adams State, Colorado, and CSIC rivals Fort Hays and Pittsburg. After a dual victory over Pittsburg and a win over Hays and Pitt in the Emporia Invitational, the Hornets finished 2nd to the host school in the Oklahoma Christian Invitational. Because of these outstanding early season performances, the Hornet harriers earned a 3rd place national ranking in the NAIA poll. However, the Tigers of Fort Hays were also ranked high in the NAIA as they once again fielded a powerful team, and one week after the Oklahoma meet, Fort Hays nipped the Hornets 26-29 in a dual meet. This loss started a string of five consecutive Hornet losses to the Tigers, as the E-State harriers finished 2nd to Hays in the Marymount Invitational, 3rd to Hays and Marymount in the Kansas Intercollegiate, and 2nd to Hays in the CSIC and District 10 meets. However, the 2nd place CSIC finish was the best in the conference meet by a Hornet team in 10 years, while the 2nd place finish in the district qualified the Hornet squad for the NAIA national meet. Unfortunately, the Hornets' hopes of a top 10

Dennis Delmott: Coach

Dennis Delmott, the former Hornet distance runner and Delavan's previous graduate assistant, was hired to coach the cross country and track teams for the 1978-79 year. Delmott earned All-American honors by finishing among the top 12 runners in the nation in 1968 and 1960. He finished in the top 25 at the U.S. Olympic Marathon Trials in 1976.

national finish went unfulfilled, as the team could manage to place only 27th. Topham led the E-State team during the season, and placed 3rd in the CSIC and district meets behind Lonnie Gee and Fred Tornedon of Hays. Rob Harber also garnered All-District honors with a 14th place finish in the district. Topham ended the year with a 34th place finish at Kenosha, Wisconsin, in the NAIA meet. Other Hornets competing at the NAIA were Harber in 195th, McPhee, in 232nd, Noonan in 236th, North in 275th , Ransom in 278th, and Gary Plank 315th.

1979

Bill Tidwell took over the job of head track and cross country coach after the 1979 track season ended, replacing Delmott who had served as interim coach for one year. Tidwell, like Delmott had done the previous year, inherited a strong cross country team in 1979. Four men who had consistently placed as scoring runners for the strong 1978 team returned, including Greg Topham and Robbie Harber, the top two runners during 1978. The Hornets were ranked among the NAIA's top 15 during most of the season, but once again, so were the Tigers of Fort Hays. The Emporia State harriers finished 6th in the Wichita Gold Classic behind four major colleges and Hays, and finished 2nd to the Tigers in the Emporia Invitational, the Hays dual, the CSIC meet and the District 10. The Hornets did not have a strong performance at the conference meet, and tied for 2nd with Kearney State behind the champion Tigers. However, at the district meet the week after the CSIC, the E-State runners performed very well, particularly Topham and Harber, in finishing 2nd to Hays. In previous years, this placing would have earned the Hornets a trip to the National meet but, unfortunately, the NAIA had reduced the number of qualifiers per district and only the district champion Tigers were able to attend nationals. Topham qualified as an individual with a 2nd place finish at districts behind Curt Shelman of Hays, but Harber just missed qualifying, finishing 6th in 24:59, only five seconds behind 5th place. Topham ended his senior cross country season placing 31st in the national meet with a time of 25:56 on the Kenosha, Wisconsin, 5-mile course. Fort Hays finished 7th in the NAIA meet, and Kearney State, the team ESU had tied with in the CSIC meet, placed 11th.

Bill Tidwell: Coach

Bill Tidwell became the cross country/track and field coach in 1979. Tidwell, the top middle distance performer in the history of Hornet track, had served as chairperson of the division of HPERA at Emporia State since 1971, but had resigned that position in January of 1979 and asked for reassignment within the division. Tidwell had been mentioned as a possible successor to Fran Welch when the great Hornet mentor had retired in 1965, but was not interested in the position at that time. Before coming to Emporia State in 1971 from Oberlin College in Ohio, Tidwell had been offered the head track and field job at Drake University but had declined the position.

1980

The 1980 cross country season was a rebuilding year for the Hornet men, as graduation had claimed six of the top seven runners from the 1979 team. Senior Kevin Byrne was the only varsity returnee, and an early season injury limited his effectiveness throughout the entire season. The youth and inexperience were quite evident during the season, and the Hornet men ended the frustrating year placing 4th in a four-team CSIC field. Steve Hawkins led the Hornets at the conference meet, finishing 19th in 25:26, with Dave Dilks 21st, Bryan Christensen 23rd, Doug Jennings 24th, Tony Wichman 25th, Kevin Byrne 26th, and Mike Avery 28th. Hawkins led the Hornets at the Salina District 10 meet running 19:12, followed by Jennings in 29:32, Wichman in 20:13, Christensen in 30:45, and Avery in 31:24.

1981

The Hornet men began to show improvement during the 1981 cross country season. After a slow start, the young E-State harriers developed into a solid team, gaining 3rd place finishes in the Marymount Invitational and Fort Hays Invitational, the last two competitions before the conference meet. Steve Hawkins led the Hornet effort by placing in the top 10 at Marymount, followed by Bob Akins in 14th and Mike Mosier in 15th. Unfortunately, late season injuries to the two top runners, juniors Hawkins and Mosier, led to low finishes in both the CSIC and District 10 meets, souring what had been a good season. At conference, Akins placed 12th in 27:19, finishing ahead of Hawkins for the first time all season, as Hawkins finished 13th in 27:32. At District 10, ESU ran without their top two runners, Hawkins and Mike Mosier, and finished last of seven teams.

1982

Disaster struck the 1982 men's cross country team, as injuries and illness destroyed what had been high hopes for a competitive season. Senior Steve Hawkins was the first casualty, missing the first half of the season with a hand injury that required surgery. Senior Mike Mosier went down next as mononucleosis removed him from competition for the entire season. Sophomore Jon Beeman was hampered all season by an illness, and freshman Kirk Porter, also a top five runner for ESU, missed the latter half of the season with an ankle injury. Beeman led the Hornets at the WSU Gold Classic and the Southwestern Invitational. Akins was the top Hornet runner at the home Emporia State Invitational, running 27:40 over the 5-mile course as the team finished 5th of five teams. Tony Wichman finished as the top ESU runner at the Pitt State meet. Because of all the health problems, the Hornets had a disappointing cross country season, which ended with only one E-State runner competing in the District 10 meet. Wichman finished 27th in 27:46 at the District 10 meet. No CSIC meet was held because of a lack of the mandatory five schools competing.

Bill Tidwell Era

The 1984 track season marked the end of Bill Tidwell's career as head coach of the Hornet teams. Tidwell moved back into an administrative position left vacant by a retirement. During his five years as coach, the men's cross country program struggled but the women's program blossomed into one of the strongest in the NAIA, as evidenced by high team places in the national meets including a runner-up national finish.

1982 cross country team

1983

The 1983 men's cross country team avoided the injury problems that had plagued the Hornets during the two previous fall seasons and posted the most successful results since 1979. Tony Wichman led the Hornets in the first two meets of the season at Wichita State and Pittsburg. Kirk Porter stepped up to the number one team position at the ESU Invitational, placing 9th in 28:25, as ESU finished 3rd of seven teams. After a slow start, Jon Beeman ran as the number one runner Hornet for the last five meets of the season, finishing 8th at the CSIC meet which was held in Emporia. ESU finished 3rd of four teams at the CSIC.

The E-State harriers ended the year placing 4th in the district meet with Beeman in 15th place, running 27:15 for the 5-mile campus course.

1984

The E-State men's cross country team opened the fall of 1984 with a new coach. Former E-State cross country and track athlete, Mark Stanbrough, took over the coaching duties. Stanbrough returned to his alma mater eager to continue the tradition of excellence the ESU men's cross country program had established.

Mark Stanbrough: Coach

Mark Stanbrough became the sixth coach in ESU men's cross country history. Stanbrough had competed in cross country and track and field for the Hornets from 1977 under Coach Phil Delavan. After graduation, he was an ESU graduate assistant in track and cross country, then taught and coached at Glasco High School for two years. He obtained his Ph.D. in exercise physiology from the University of Oregon. While in Oregon, Stanbrough competed for Athletes in Action and the Oregon Track Club.

The 1984 men returned only three lettermen from the previous season. It was a year filled with injuries. The Hornets were unable to field a full team during the season until the CSIC meet. Justin Combes led E-State at the conference meet with a 13th place finish in 27:37 over the 5-mile course, as the Hornets finished a distant 4th of four teams. Kirk Porter in 15th (27:50), Steve Peterson in 17th (28:05), Richard Cox in 22nd, and Jerry Daniel in 26th, completed the ESU team. The Hornets finished 6th in the District 10 meet with Combes again leading the way for the Hornets with a 25th place finish in in 28:30.

1985

Needing to build both quantity and quality, Stanbrough had recruited heavily for the 1985 season. One of the top recruits was Roger Jennings from Phillipsburg, Kansas. Jennings was a state placer at Phillipsburg, placing 2nd in the 3A 3200 meters. His top high school time in the 1600 was 4:28 and as he matured as a runner, he would eventually lower his time to the equivalent of a sub-4 minute mile (1500 conversion) while at ESU. Jennings arrived as a raw runner with tremendous potential. His dad was the long-time coach/manager of the Pacific Coast Track Club (one of the top clubs in the U.S. with Dwight Stones and Al Feuerbach as athletes) and his step dad was the legendary John Mason, who ran for Fort Hays and later the Pacific Coast Club. Mason ran numerous miles under 4 minutes and won two national

NAIA cross country titles and eight NAIA national track and field titles. One of the reasons Jennings was attracted to ESU was the fact that he was familiar with the name of Feuerbach. Feuerbach was a member of the Pacific Coast, the same club that Jennings' dad, Tom, coached and managed. Feuerbach competed at Emporia State, winning four NAIA National Championships before making two Olympic teams and setting a world record in the shot put. Jennings started his college running career at the Wichita State Gold Classic and led the Hornets to a 2nd place university team finish, the start of an illustrious career that culminated in two individual national championships and two national runner-up finishes on the track. Jennings placed 18th at Wichita State, followed by the tight pack of newcomers Eric Baumgartel, Paul Weidenbach, Greg Burger, and David Gehrke.

Jennings would again lead the men the following week at the Kansas Invitational with fellow freshman Heath Cheatham running second man and freshman Weidenbach running 3rd man. For the freshmen, it was the first 10K of their young careers. The Hornets finished 4th behind Kansas, Nebraska, and Pittsburg State, who had the individual champion in Irishman Willie Walsh.

Running at the home ESU Invitational in a large field of 12 teams, ESU finished 5th. Mark Feldkamp led the way with a 27:33 followed by Cheatham in 27:39, and Jennings back at 28:07 for the 5-mile distance on a muddy course. The Swede Invitational hosted by Bethany College and held at the Lindsborg golf course was an outstanding meet drawing the top NAIA teams from Kansas and Nebraska, as well as some junior colleges. Growing NAIA power Southwestern dominated the meet, placing five runners in the top 12. The Hornets finished 6th in the 14-team field. Gehrke led the Hornets, running 27:24, with Burger three seconds back and Peterson following in 27:41. Burger and Peterson were high school teammates at Axtell coached by former ESU running standout, Tom Noonan, an All-District and national qualifier performer. Cloud County Community College transfer Dennis Cargill and Eric Baumgartel closed out the scoring with the Hornets achieving a tight 13-second time gap between the 1st and 6th place runners.

The young Hornets started to gain confidence with a 2nd place finish at the Marymount College Invitational. With 11 teams represented, ESU finished 2nd behind Kansas State, 47-70. Although not as tight of a pack as the week before, the time gap between runners 1-7 was less than one minute. Jennings again led the Hornets with a top 10 finish, with Gehrke beginning to establish himself as a consistent runner.

ESU traveled to the University of Arkansas, a program that had established one of the great traditions in college cross country. The Hornets finished 6th of the six scoring teams in the 10K behind Arkansas, Arkansas Alumni, Colorado, Oklahoma and Oklahoma State. Olympian Joe Falcon won, with the Hornets' top runner Cheatham back in 37th place.

> **Former Hornet John McDonnell: Winningest Coach in NCAA History**
>
> Coach John McDonnell of the Arkansas Razorbacks became the winningest coach in NCAA history, all sports, with 40 national titles. McDonnell, a native Irishman, had started his illustrious career running for the Hornets in 1964, earning double All-American honors at the NAIA National Championships, placing 2nd in the 1500 and 3rd in the 3000 meter steeplechase. He ran one semester before transferring to Southwestern Louisiana.
>
>

The CSIC meet at Kearney State was a Pittsburg State affair with the Gorillas dominating the meet. Peterson, Cheatham, and Gehrke led the Hornets in 10th, 11th, and 12th. Baumgartel in 14th and Weidenbach in 16th completed the scoring, as ESU finished 3rd in the four-team field. The District 10 meet at Hays served as a qualifying meet for the NAIA national meet. Based upon the success of the high team placings of the District 10 teams the previous year at the NAIA national meet, three national qualifying berths were available. The competition turned out to be one of many battles. The battle of the cold environmental conditions consisted of 25-degree temperatures and a north wind of 15 miles per hour. The second fight was the team battle-actually two different battles. The first battle was between Southwestern and Pittsburg, with Southwestern winning the team title, 30-33. The other team battle was between Emporia State, Fort Hays, and Bethany for the final qualifying spot. Freshman Gehrke, who had turned into one of ESU's most consistent runners, led the way for ESU in 26:12 and a 18th place finish, with fellow freshman Weidenbach finishing 19th. The Hornets came out 16 points ahead of Fort Hays to qualify for nationals as a team for the first time in seven years.

ESU finished in 28th place as a team at the 1985 NAIA National Cross Country Championships with the team finishing in the following order: Jennings, Feldkamp, Gehrke, Weidenbach, Peterson, Cargill, and Burger. Counting the three individual women runners ESU qualified, plus the seven men, the contingent was the largest ESU national representation in cross country history. With 22 of the 24 members of the ESU men's and women's cross country teams new to the program, the future looked bright as the Hornets were determined to maintain the legendary cross country history.

1986

After qualifying for the NAIA national meet the year before, the 1986 men's cross country team opened with high hopes for the season at the Wichita State Gold Classic. Roger Jennings, who was coming off a very successful track season, placed 3rd in 26:11 to take two minutes off his previous best cross country time. Jason Schenck, who was the 10th man a year earlier, moved up to the number two man and finished 22nd. Freshman James Hardy debuted in 36th place, as the team finished 4th.

The season continued at the Kansas University Invitational, where the men battled a hilly course to take home a 6th place finish behind KU, Southwest Missouri, and Drake. Jennings dropped out of the race midway through the run due to a foot injury and Schenck ran the 10K course in 34:59 to lead the Hornets. Jennings returned the following week winning the 5-mile Emporia Invitational race in 27:29. Schenck again ran 2nd for the Hornets and Mark Feldkamp ran strong as ESU's third runner. At the Marymount College Invitational, Jennings tried a different strategy. A strong 1500 man on the track, his usual strategy was to sit back and move late in the race with a strong kick. However, he changed strategies and ran hard from the start to control the race and win by 15 seconds, leading ESU to a second place team finish behind national power Southwestern. Jennings continued his hot streak at the Bethany Invitational the following week. His time of 26:15 equaled his season best and Schenck continued to be consistent, finishing 11th individually to help lead the Hornets to a 4th place showing. The following week at the Pittsburg State Invitational, Jennings finished second, covering the 5-mile course in a fast 25:08 leading the men to another 2nd place finish behind Southwestern.

The Hornets were looking for their first conference title in 23 years as they competed in the CSIC Championships at Pittsburg State. Although Jennings again led the men with a 2nd place finish in 25:25, Fort Hays edged ESU by a mere two points, 30-32. Emporia State waited only a week for revenge against the Tigers of Fort Hays. With a national berth on the line, the Hornets edged the Tigers by a single point at the District 10 meet. Despite finishing 2nd behind Southwestern, ESU garnered a coveted national qualifying spot. Jennings finished in 25:10, 10 seconds back of the winner, Cormic O'Riordan of Pittsburg State. Schenk and Weidenbach also earned All-District 10 honors finishing 11th in 26:28 and 13th in 26:36, respectively. At the NAIA National Cross Country Championships, the men finished 22nd, their highest national finish in 11 years. Jennings improved on his previous year's national performance by more than three minutes to finish 39th in 25:53 on the 8000-meter course. The other Hornets were Weidenbach in 127th at 26:24, Peterson in 186th at 26:52, Schenck in 219th at 27:12, Feldkamp in 222nd at 27:14, Burger in 227th at 27:17, and Rod Taylor in 298th at 28:17. Despite the men's best national finish in years, the Lady Hornets' 2nd place finish at nationals overshadowed the men's team accomplishment.

1987

Slowed by injuries and illness, the men struggled to establish a rhythm in 1987. After runner-up finishes in the conference and district meets the previous year, the men fell to 3rd and 4th in 1987. Highlights of the season included 2nd place finishes in the Swede and Pittsburg Invitationals.

Jennings was the Hornets' number one man every time out and near the front in every race. Jennings ran outstanding races to win the CSIC meet and the Swede Invite individual title, but faltered at districts and failed to qualify for the national meet. Jennings ran with the lead pack at the Swede Invite for four miles, and then buried the field with an impressive finish over the final mile. The ESU junior, an All-American miler on the track, finished in 24:50, followed by Cargill in 7th at 25:33. Scott Starks was 24th in 26:27, Wade Caselman 30th in 26:41, and Weidenbach 32nd with a 26:48. The Hornets took 2nd in the team results. At the CSIC, Jennings dueled with Pittsburg State's standout Allan Peyton, a freshman from Ireland. Peyton had defeated Jennings four previous times over the course of the season, but Jennings had narrowed the gap every time and was determined not to lose the CSIC race on home turf and to an Irishman from Pittsburg for the third consecutive year. PSU's Irishman Willie Walsh (1985) and Cormac O'Riordan (1986) had won the last two conference titles.

Jennings and Peyton made the men's race strictly a two-person chase from the beginning. At the 3-mile mark, they had built a 30-second lead on the rest of the field with Jennings sitting on Peyton's shoulder. Jennings told the Emporia Gazette, "I'm definitely a leech, more or less," Jennings said of his race strategy. "That's how I always run track. I don't like to lead too much, it feels like I'm alone out there." But with three-quarters of a mile remaining, Jennings turned on his All-American miler's speed and Peyton could only watch as Jennings won, going away in 25:37, while Peyton was a distant 2nd in 25:57. Cargill ran number two man for the Hornets much of the season and that is where he ran at the conference meet, despite being a little over-excited and leading the race early, going out a little too fast in his last conference cross country race and fading to 11th in 27:40. Caselman placed 14th in 27:58 and Starks was 18th in 27:58, as the Hornets finished 3rd behind Fort Hays and Pittsburg State.

At the District 10 meet at Pittsburg State, Jennings could only manage a 9th place finish in 26:06 and failed to qualify for an individual berth in the NAIA national meet. Conference runner-up Peyton of Pittsburg State won the individual title (he went on to earn All-American honors by placing 22nd at nationals) covering the 5 miles in 25:17. Jennings was the only top-20 performer with Starks next in 21st at 27:06 and Caselman 32nd in 27:30. Starks and Caselman ran numbers three and four for the majority of the season and contributed significantly to the team. However, the fifth man for the Hornets varied each meet and also affected the Hornets season dramatically. Upperclassmen that were to be a key to a successful season were injured or ill much of the season.

1988

National 1500-meter champion Roger Jennings had competed in Europe over the summer and was held out of the early meets of the 1988 men's cross country season. The Hornets, running without their front-runner, started off the season at the WSU Gold Classic and finished 3rd in the team standings lead by Brad Wecker, a freshman and state cross country champion from Emporia High, placing 18th in 26:56. Wecker also led the Hornets at the Mid-America Nazarene Invitational by winning the competition in 28:03 followed by Starks in 7th place in 29:13 as the Hornets placed 2nd as a team. Jennings returned for the ESU Invitational to place 4th in 25:52 behind three Kansas State runners. Wecker followed close behind in sixth in 26:11, with Starks making the top 20 in 16th place at 27:46. ESU finished third as a team. Jennings led the Hornets with a third place finish at the Swede Invitational running a quick 25:28, with Wecker again close behind in 25:55 in 6th as the Hornets finished 4th. ESU added a 2nd place team finish at the Pittsburg and Southwestern Invites, again led by Jennings and Wecker.

The 'Chunky Kids' Win First Conference Title in 25 years

The Hornets competed in the 1988 CSIC Cross Country Championships at Fort Hays State University in 40-50 mile per hour winds. The top four teams all finished within 4 points of each other but ESU captured the title, their first conference title in 25 years. Fort Hays State coach Jim Krob was quoted in The Hays Daily News as saying, "The tall, skinny guys really had to fight the wind. Emporia has little chunky kids and a couple of horses that handled the conditions well." The horses, as they had been all year, were Jennings and Wecker, and the Emporia twosome finished 3rd and 4th, respectively.

The 1988 CSIC title was one of the closest team battles in the history of the conference. Although only four teams were competing in the conference, the quality was outstanding as Emporia State's competition in the meet would all go on to finish in the top 20 at the national meet with Pittsburg State finishing 9th, Kearney State 14th, and Fort Hays 18th. The meet was held at Fort Hays State on the college campus as the runners battled a stiff 40 to 50 mile-per-hour north wind. Only four points separated the four teams competing. ESU posted 52 points to edge Fort Hays by one point with Pittsburg 3rd at 54 and Kearney 4th with 56 points. The Hornets were elated to capture the title, as it was their first conference title in 25 years for the men's cross country team. Jennings and Wecker finished 3rd and 4th, respectively, to help lead ESU to the coveted conference title. Completing the scoring were Starks in 7th, Caselman in 18th, and Clint Burkdoll in 20th.

The following week, both Pittsburg and Fort Hays turned the table on ESU with the Hornets finishing 4th at District 10 and failing to qualify as a team for nationals. Brendan Murphy of Pittsburg State won the race in 25:15, followed by Jennings in 25:35, ahead of his old nemesis Peyton of Pitt State (who went on to earn another All-American honor with an 18th place national finish). Wecker placed 10th, Starks 15th,

Caselman 33rd, and Tom Grady 34th. Although he qualified as an individual representative to the NAIA National Cross Country meet, Jennings, the national 1500-meter champion elected to not to participate to focus on preparing for the upcoming track season.

1989

Although the Hornets had lost NAIA Track and Field All-Americans Roger Jennings and Scott Starks, they returned some solid performers and added David Kipelio. Kipelio, a native Kenyan was a transfer from Southwestern Louisiana. After transferring to ESU, staying healthy and able to accumulate a good foundation of training miles, Kipelio began to gain confidence and won the NAIA national steeplechase title in the spring of 1989. He competed in Finland over the summer and was ready for a successful cross country and track season. The season started at the Wichita State Gold Classic. To give Kipelio more recovery from his summer track season in Finland, he did not compete in the first meet. In their Hornet debuts, three newcomers paced the attack. Steve Clum picked up an 8th place showing (17:15) and Hutchinson Community College transfer Matt Hertig was 16th, with freshman Todd Allen in 18th. At the Kansas University Invitational, freshman Clum again led the Hornets with a 15th place finish in 26:53. Kipelio made his debut at the Maple Leaf Invitational at Baker University and immediately established his presence, leaving the field behind early and taking the title in 25:14. ESU, keying off Kipelio, established position early and passed several runners over the last mile to place five runners in the top 10 for the win with Hertig 4th, Clum 6th, Boyle 8th, and Allen 10th.

Kipelio, in his second cross country race, outclassed the field to win by a minute at the ESU Invitational. Kipelio bided his time early, and when the pace slowed, he took off around the halfway mark and never looked back, winning in 25:38. The Hornets put four in the top 10 led by Hertig, Allen, and Caselman to win over Hutchinson by the score of 27-41. Kipelio continued to be the class of the field at the Swede invitational at Bethany, although his winning time of 25:39 could not pull the Hornets to the win, as they finished 3rd.

ESU competed in a unique and enjoyable relay race in 1989 called the *Ekedin* relay. The Japanese term originally referred to a stagecoach that transmitted communication by stages. The concept involves runners racing relay legs of various lengths, a nice break from traditional cross country racing. The women raced legs of 1 mile-2 mile-1 mile with the men racing miles of 1-2-3-2-1. Tom Grady's lead-off leg put the Hornets in front and a quick 3 mile by Kipelio put the win away for ESU.

The Hornets traditionally used the Southwestern Invitational as a final tune-up before the conference and district meets. With a flat and fast course, the Hornets had fared well in the past. 1989 would be no exception as ESU finished 2nd, beating 8th nationally-ranked Oklahoma Baptist, but falling to Southwestern. The race featured a dual between Kipelio and Oklahoma Baptist's national contender, Peter Schouw. The two ran together for 4.5 miles before Kipelio pulled away in the last half-mile to win in 24:42. Boyle added to the team effort by finishing in the top 10.

With the CSIC disbanded, the Hornets did not have a conference meet in 1989 and turned their focus on the District 10 meet. Returning to the course they had won the Baker Invitational on earlier in the year, the men ran into a buzzsaw in the form of Southwestern and Fort Hays. The Hornets saw their season end by placing 3rd, as only the top two teams qualified for national meet. Kipelio dominated the race from the

31

mile mark on to win individual honors for the men to qualify as an individual and Matt Hertig added a 12th place finish to earn All-District honors.

Kipelio entered the NAIA national meet undefeated but faced a tough field, including two-time defending champion Rick Robirds of Adams State. Kipelio finished 21st at the NAIA Nationals and was the first Hornet harrier since Greg Purkeypile turned the trick in 1976 to become an All-American. Robirds won for his third straight year to lead Adams State to the team title. With the temperature at 20 degrees and windy, the conditions were not ideal, nor Kenya-like. Kipelio never could find his rhythm and had an off-race compared to his consistent front-running he had displayed all year. Peter Schouw of Oklahoma Baptist, whom Kipelio had defeated just a few weeks earlier, finished 3rd.

1990

With national champion steeplechaser David Kipelio out of cross country eligibility, the team took on a new look. Brad Wecker returned for his senior year and Rick Boyle established himself as a team front-runner. Early in the season, the men tied for the team title at Pittsburg State led by the 7th of Boyle in 25:51, the 12th place finish of Allen in 26:37, and the 13th and 14th of Hertig and Tim Bartz, respectively. Boyle again led the team in a fast 26:05 at Missouri Southern, with Hertig running 26:14 to lead ESU to a 5th place finish out of 23 teams behind the champion—the legendary Arkansas program.

David Kipelio: All-American

David Kipelio was a three-time NAIA National Champion, twice in the steeplechase and once in the indoor two mile. He was a nine-time All-American in track and once in cross country finishing 21st. He set four school records, the indoor 3000 and 5000 and the outdoor steeplechase and 5000 meters.

ESU defended home turf by winning the Emporia Invitational, defeating 15 teams and fielded a second team of junior varsity runners that finished 5th. The Hornets put seven runners in the top 12 with Boyle in 2nd at 25:58; 3rd, Shawn Thomas in 26:23; 5th, Allen in 26:36; 8th, Wecker in 26:48; 9th, Bartz in 26:59; 11th, Grady at 27:07; 12th, Caselman, at 27:19. Competing in the always tough Swede Invite, the men finished 5th, led by the 2nd place finish of Rick Boyle in 26:41, with Bartz following in 27:55.

ESU journeyed to Kenosha, Wisconsin during the middle of the season to run on the national cross country course and prepare for the national competition later in the year. ESU finished 7th of 23 teams led by Boyle in 22nd at 26:48, Hertig was 52nd, and Allen 60th. The Southwestern Invite was a tight team battle with ESU placing 3rd only 8 points away from the title. Allen led the way in 13th with a 26:29, Wecker 16th in 26:35, Hertig 20th in 26:45, and Boyle 22nd in 26:50.

For the second year in a row, ESU was not in a conference and therefore was not able to compete in a conference meet, so the team championship focus was on the District 10 meet. ESU finished 3rd behind

Southwestern and Fort Hays as ESU failed to qualify for nationals as a team. Brad Wecker led the team with a 7th place finish in 26:58. Hertig was 10th and Boyle finished 13th in rainy, very windy conditions at 38 degrees. Wecker's effort qualified him as an individual for the NAIA national meet, where he finished 149th in 27:10 in a field of 358 finishers.

1991

The 1991 cross country season started with high hopes for a great season. Two seniors were scheduled to lead the way. Alberto Lopez, a transfer from Blinn Community College, was highly decorated before arriving at ESU. At Blinn, he was the National Junior College indoor two-mile champion, but his greatest honor was competing in the 1984 Olympic Games in Los Angeles, California. Competing for his home country of Guatemala, he ran in both the 400 meters and 800 meters. He made his presence felt at ESU in the spring of 1991 as he anchored the Hornets' winning distance medley relay team at the Drake Relays and also ran on the winning 4 x 800 team. The other senior, Rick Boyle, had established himself by finishing 8th in the national indoor 3-mile run. The previous cross country season, he had led the Hornets as the number one runner before being hampered by injuries. Unfortunately, Boyle, who had been injury plagued his entire career, suffered a season-ending injury before

> **Alberto Lopez: Olympian**
> Alberto Lopez ran for the Hornets in 1991. A transfer from Blinn Community College, Lopez ran for his native country of Guatemala in the 1984 Olympic Games in Los Angeles. Lopez ran athe 400 clocking a 52.21 for 8th in his heat and the 800 meters, where he ran 1:54.19 and finished 6th in his heat. Lopez was a national junior college champion at two miles. Lopez ran on two victorious relays at the Drake Relays, anchoring the distance medley.

the season even started. Lopez was also met with difficulties before the start of the season and had to return home to Guatemala. With the addition of Shawn Thomas, an All-American at 10K for Allen County Community College, and significant improvement from numerous team members, the loss of the top two runners for the Hornets was offset.

The season started at Pittsburg State on a flat and fast course. Newcomer Thomas made an immediate impact, winning the 8K race in 25:52 with teammate Gary Lyles finishing a close 2nd in 26:12. The 1-2 punch led to a 2nd place finish. Thomas led the team the next week at Missouri Southern, blasting the fast course in 24:34, finishing 15th in a loaded field, including perennial national NCAA champion Arkansas. Four Hornets broke 26 minutes with Thomas, Gary Lyles, Richard Mick, and Wecker under the barrier. Lyles, a transfer from Barton County, was starting to gain momentum and that carried over the next week at the Emporia Invite. In the 13-team field, the Hornets captured the title led by Lyles's 2nd place finish and placed five men in the top 10. The Hornets displayed great team depth as they ran without Thomas, but got a 5th place finish out of Andrew LaRouche. LaRouche was a pleasant surprise as a walk-on. He came to ESU as an exchange student from Lasungu Malawi, Africa, but he also had dual citizenship as a Canadian.

Coach Stanbrough's philosophy, excellent competition would make you better, brought the Hornets to the Oklahoma State Cowboy Jamboree and the Arkansas Invitational. In Arkansas, the competition was top-notch, with NCAA champion Arkansas and NAIA champion Lubbock Christian, as well as five Big 8 teams. The Hornets remained on track with PRs for everyone on the 10K course. Leading into the District 10 meet, ESU picked up a win at the Southwestern Invitation with six Hornets-Thomas, Lyles, LaRouche, Mick, Wecker, and Bartz-all under 26:20.

With a national berth on the line, the 1991 harriers hosted the district meet in Emporia. Sub-zero wind chill conditions did not deter the determined efforts, as ESU captured their first men's NAIA District 10 Championship in history (the meet was implemented in 1970). The Hornets put five men in the top nine to win easily over traditional powerhouse Southwestern. Lyles led the effort with a 2nd place finish followed by Thomas, Mick, Wecker, and LaRouche with a strong, team-oriented 48-second time gap.

When the Hornets appeared at the 1991 national meet in Kenosha, Wisconsin, they faced a hilly, muddy course. The Hornet effort led to a 5th place finish, their best national finish since 1968 when the Hornets were 2nd at the National Championships. Lyles earned All-American Honors in 16th place (25:26). Following Lyles were Thomas in 35th (25:53), Mick in 38th (25:56), and LaRouche in 49th (26:14). Mick stepped up to the occasion and ran his best race of the year. He had started his career earlier at ESU and then transferred to Kansas State. After a year at Kansas State, he was back at ESU and the Hornets benefitted from his talents. LaRouche, the walk-on,

---

Gary Lyles: All-American

Gary Lyles was the final NAIA All-American for Emporia State when he finished 16th at Kenosha, Wisconsin in 1991. Lyles led the team to a 5th place team finish, their highest finish in 23 years. Lyles finished 2nd to lead the 1991 men to their first ever District 10 cross country title in the 21 year history of District 10 competition.

---

would continue to improve and return to future success at the national meet and earn All-American honors. Rounding out the national team was Wecker in 122nd at (27:08) and Colby Smith in 260th (28:37).

The 1991 cross country season also marked the end of the Stanbrough-coached era, as he stepped down after he led ESU through eight successful seasons.

NAIA Legendary Program

The 1991 cross country season signaled the end of the NAIA era for Emporia State. The NAIA started national cross country meets in 1956. ESU's legendary Bill Tidwell competed in the first NAIA meet, finishing 2nd and leading the men to a 4th place team finish. The inaugural meet was just the beginning of a very successful NAIA cross country tradition at Emporia State. The Hornet harriers claimed NAIA cross country championships in 1958, 1959, 1961, and 1962. They won a NCAA small college title in 1963. They finished as the NAIA national runner-up 1963, 1964, and 1968. Ireland Sloan in 1962 and John Camien in 1963 and 1964 won individual NAIA National Championships. Sixteen men earned NAIA Cross Country All-American honors in the 28-year history of Emporia State's association with the NAIA.

1992

David Harris was hired to lead the ESU program beginning in 1992 as ESU moved to the NCAA Division II level of competition and joined the Mid-America Intercollegiate Athletics Association.

The 1992 cross country season and the Harris era began at the WSU Gold Classic, with ESU 3rd behind K-State and Oklahoma State. Returners Thomas and LaRouche led the way with Thomas 9th in 20:46, LaRouche 12th, Jesse Griffin 20th, Donald Palmer 24th, and Bartz 25th. The team finished 5th at the always challenging Missouri Southern Stampede behind the 18th place of Thomas in 25:14.

Mark Stanbrough Era

While head coach cross country coach for the men's and women's cross country teams, Stanbrough led the women's team to a runner-up national finish in 1986 and captured five District 10 titles in his eight year tenure. The men's team completed their highest national finish in 1991 placing 5th. The 1991 team also won the District 10 for the first time in the 21 years it had been held and the 1988 team won their first conference title in 24 years.

He coached seven cross country All-Americans. He coached 28 Athletes to 60 NAIA All-American Honors, including 11 National Champions in track and field/cross country. He coached 10 teams that finished in the top 10 in the nation and 22 teams that finished in the top 20 in national competition.

Thomas picked up a win at the ESU Invitational, but it was not without some controversy. Butler County's Jermaine Mitchell led comfortably from the start to the finish but was disqualified for inadvertently leaving the course and shaving approximately 150 meters off the run. Mitchell's disqualification left runner-up Thomas as the winner and added 39 points to Butler County's team total, dropping the Grizzlies from 1st to 3rd. Thomas had finished 45 seconds behind Mitchell, but in the new results, he took the win by 12 seconds. LaRouche was 6th, Griffin 7th, Bartz 13th, and Palmer 19th. Ironically, Mitchell didn't hold the disqualification against ESU, as he

NCAA

After 35 years, ESU also moved to the NCAA Division II level of competition and joined the Mid-America Intercollegiate Athletics Association.

transferred the following year to ESU and became one of the great distance runners in ESU history.

With the move to the NCAA DII, ESU was now in the MIAA conference, and in 1992, they made their conference debut a successful one with a 3rd place team finish. Thomas finished 3rd, only six seconds behind the winner Rob Jenson of Northeast Missouri. Thomas was running in second most of the race but exerted a high amount of energy trying to reel in Jenson and was passed by a late surge. However, Thomas set a personal best at 24:22 and was followed by LaRouche in 6th (24:59), Griffin in 18th (25:58), Palmer in 20th (25:03), and Bartz in 23rd (26:15).

Thomas, Emporia's top harrier throughout the year, finished 5th in the Great Lakes Regional Championships in Big Rapids, Michigan. Thomas completed the 10K course in 31:47 to barely miss an individual qualifying berth as two conference competitors he had beaten the meet before finished ahead of him, earning individual berths. LaRouche finished in 10th with a time of 33:10. The men's team finished 5th, one point behind Pittsburg State. E-State and Pittsburg ran against each other three times on the season with the Gorillas winning all three contests by a total of five points.

1993

Jermaine Mitchell, the transfer from Butler County, led the Hornets to a season-opening 2nd place team finish at the Wichita State Gold Classic with a 5th place finish. Mitchell won the ESU Invite with a 26:11 over the 5-mile course (after having been disqualified the year before on the course when he ran for Butler County) and led the Hornets to the team title. The Hornets finished 3rd

David Harris: Coach
David Harris was hired to lead the ESU program. Harris came to ESU after a seven-year stint as an assistant coach at the University of Nebraska where he coached 31 All-American and three Olympians. Harris received his bachelor's degree in physical education/social science and a master's degree in athletic administration from Northeast Missouri State University. While competing for the Bulldogs, he was a four-year letterman in cross country and track and field.

in the MIAA meet, led by LaRouche, who finished 2nd in 25:18.7, with teammates following in 11th (Chris Koppenhaver), 14th (Jason Hendry), 19th (Erik Clarr), and 43rd (Ed O'Malley). Mitchell was leading the race before dropping out.

At the Great Lakes Regional meet, Mitchell ran the 10K in 30:27 to win and the Hornets finished 3rd to qualify for the NCAA Cross Country Championships. The national meet was held in California at the Victoria Country Club in Riverside, California. The team finished 12th but the distance was unknown. A detour taken by 123 runners shaved about 1000 meters off the steepest portion of the course. The misdirection started when the leaders neared the golf course's eighth hole. The route called for runners to veer left up an embankment. Flags marked the way, and a course official stood about 100 yards earlier, but there was no monitor at the turn. Thus, when the runners approached and lost their bearing, there was no one to ask. Only five of the 128 runners ran the correct course and those five took five of the last six places in the 10,000-meter race.

Wrong Way
At the 1993 National Cross Country meet held in Riverside, California, 123 of 128 the participants took a wrong turn on the course and ran 1,000 meters short. Only five of the 128 runners ran the correct course and they took five of the last six places in the 10,000 meter race. Two ESU runners, Jason Hendry and Ed O'Malley, were part of the last five. Technically, the runners who cut distance off the course should have been disqualified which would have moved Hendry and O'Malley up into the top five.It also would have disqualified all the other 123 runners. However, no one protested so the results stood.

Mitchell and LaRouche both earned All-American honors with 15th and 20th place finishes, marking the first time since 1968 that

ESU had earned multiple All-American at the national meet. Travis Heimer in 86th, Claar in 96th, Koppenhaver in 119th, O'Malley in 126th, and Hendry in 127th completed the team.

1994

Jermaine Mitchell was establishing himself as one of the greatest distance runners in ESU history in 1994. The Jamaican led ESU in every race and started the season by winning the college division and placing 6th overall at the Jayhawk Invite in 25:00 over the 8K course. After battling injuries the previous year, sophomore Sean Bennington finished 10th with a time of 26:43. The men finished 2nd in the college division at the Woody Greeno meet in Lincoln, Nebraska with Mitchell 3rd overall, running 25:19. LaRouche finished 12th, with Koppenhaver in 13th, both breaking 27 minutes.

Andrew LaRouche: All-American
Andrew LaRouche went from a walk-on to an All-American at ESU. He finished 20th in the 1993 NCAA National Cross Country Championships. He finished 2nd in the 1992 MIAA meet. LaRouche finished 49th in the 1991 NAIA National meet to help the Hornets to a 5th place team finish.

ESU ventured to the Minnesota Invitational and finished 4th among 22 schools in the DII division. Mitchell again led the charge, breaking 25 minutes in 24:57 and finishing 3rd among DII runners. LaRouche took 13th with a time of 25:56. At the ESU Invitational, the Hornets finished in 2nd behind Central Missouri State. Mitchell took the individual title in 25:33 with McCleary in 13th at 27:00 followed by Hendry in 27:06.

Behind Mitchell's efforts the Hornets ran to a 2nd place finish in the MIAA. The race was a sweet revenge for Mitchell, who was leading the 1993 MIAA championship race before dropping out. Mitchell captured the MIAA crown by finishing the 8K race in 25:39. ESU finished 2nd with 55 points, four points behind Northeast Missouri State, which captured its second team title in three years. Following Mitchell was senior LaRouche in 3rd in 26:00, Josh McCleary in 12th, Koppenhaver in 17th, and Garth Briggeman in 22nd.

Jermaine Mitchell: All-American
Jermaine Mitchell established himself as one of the top distance runners in ESU history finishing a brilliant cross country career as a three-time All-American (tied for the second most in school history-John Camien had four) and a two-time MIAA champion. Mitchell finished 15th in 1993, 3rd in 1994, and 7th in 1996.

At the Great Lakes Regional, Mitchell was 2nd in 32:33 over the 10K course with LaRouche following in 6th in 33.22. LaRouche who had placed 20th in the national meet the previous season, just missed out by one spot on earning a berth to nationals after finishing 3rd among individuals, with the top two individuals qualifying.

Mitchell earned his second cross country All-American honor at the NCAA Division II Cross Country Championships in Kearney, Nebraska. The native of Porus, Jamaica, finished the 10K race in 31:11 to finish in 3rd place. The 3rd place finish by Mitchell was the highest cross country finish since John Camien captured the NAIA title in 1964. Mitchell became only the fifth ESU cross country runner to finish in the top three at the national cross country meet. Mitchell represented his country of Jamaica as he competed in the Caribbean Cross Country Championships, finishing 2nd in 35:06 over the 12,000-meter course to lead Jamaica to a 2nd place finish behind Mexico.

1995

1995 was a transition year as All-American Jermaine Mitchell red-shirted. Coach Harris had a very young team with two sophomores and four freshmen among his top runners. Josh McCleary stepped up as the number one man to lead ESU. The men finished in 5th at the Maple Leaf Invitational with McCleary placing 10th in 16:18. McCleary again led the team with a 9th place finish in 26:43 at the Missouri Southern Stampede as the men finished 6th, and Tye Cooley added a 10th place finish in 26:56. The ESU Invite saw the Hornets place 2nd. Again, McCleary led the way with a 3rd place effort in 26:52, with Hendry in 7th, Cooley 9th, and Chris Denton 11th.

ESU finished 4th at MIAA's with McCleary leading the way in 13th in 25:38, and Briggeman 17th in 26:07. The Great Lakes Regional meet ended the season with a 15th place team finish out of 20 scoring teams. McCleary posted the top performance with a 57th place finish in 34:20 over the 10K course. The team was young and gained experience as the season progressed, but the accumulating fatigue of the long collegiate season played a major factor in team success near the end of the season.

1996

Jermaine Mitchell returned from his redshirt year and immediately took up where he had left off. He started with a Maple Leaf 5K win in 15:26 as the team finished 3rd, with McLeary running in the number two spot, finishing 11th in 16:10. Mitchell then ran the Jayhawk Invite with a 24:53 over 8K as he finished 3rd to two University of Michigan runners. Jamin Swift ran in the number two spot for ESU, clocking 26:59, the same time as Drew Ryun, son of the legendary KU runner and former multiple world record holder, Jim Ryun. ESU finished 9th in the team competition won by Michigan with Southern Illinois 2nd and the U.S. Naval Academy 3rd. Mitchell returned to his winning ways at the SMU Invite winning in 24:47 as the men were 2nd, and Mitchell broke the line first again in the ESU Invite, winning by 30 seconds in 24:52. Swift in 13th, Tye Cooley in 20th, and Briggeman in 25th helped Emporia State to a 3rd place team finish at the ESU Invite.

Running without Mitchell at the Ollie Isom Invite (named after long time coach Ollie Isom) at Butler County, ESU posted a 2nd place finish as Swift and Briggeman again led the team in 7th and 12th. Mitchell returned to win his second MIAA cross country title, traversing the Kirksville, Missouri course in 25:01, with Swift following in 19th (26:43), and Briggeman in 22nd at 27:14. ESU finished 5th in the team competition. Mitchell lost to his first non-NCAA DI competitor of the year at the Great Lakes Regional hosted by Central Missouri. Elly Rono of Southern Indiana bested Mitchell by a mere two seconds with Mitchell running 31:25 over the 10K course. Briggeman was 45th in 34:09, followed by Swift in 62nd, Cooley in 71st, and Alan Trites in 99th.

At the 1996 NCAA DII National Cross Country Championships held in McKinleyville, California, the MIAA was well represented on the men's side. Central Missouri State finished 6th behind the national champion Alexander Alexin. Mitchell had defeated Alexin in the previous two races, both at the MIAA and the Regional meet; however, it was Alexin's day, as Mitchell finished in 7th running 31:55 for the 10K distance to end his brilliant cross country career as a three-time All-American (tied for the second most in school history-John Camien had four) and a two-time MIAA champion.

1997

The 1997 cross country team was one of transition, as Jermaine Mitchell had graduated. The team began the season at the Gold Classic at Wichita State, finishing 4th. Josh McCleary had a top 10-finish in 8th, running 21:21 for 4 miles. Emporia finished 10th overall and 2nd in the small college division in the SMU Invitational held in Dallas, Texas. McCleary again led the way with a 36th place in 27:26 and Swift running 27:59 to finish 51st.

The men finished 3rd of five scoring teams at the ESU Invite. Tye Cooley led the way with a 10th place finish in 28:29. Competing against national junior college power Butler County, ESU finished behind the host team at the Butler County Isom Invitational. Swift and McCleary finished 5-6 with Swift running 27:04.

The team ran well at the MIAA Championships, finishing 3rd, led by Swift in 11th (26:35) and McCleary 16th in 26:52. The NCAA Great Lakes Regional saw the Hornets finish in 11th, led by the 34th place finish by Swift in 33:10 over 10K and the 41st place finish of McCleary.

1998

The 1998 cross country season started off with Senior Josh McCleary leading the Hornets with an 8th place finish in 26:47 and the team to a 3rd place tie with the Shockers at the Wichita State Gold Classic. Freshman Josh Katzer finished 18th in 27:38, and Eric Meyer was 19th in 27:51. McCleary continued to lead the way with an 11th place finish at the Jayhawk Invitational and a 3rd place finish at the Cavalier Cup, as the Hornets finished 2nd as a team. In their only home meet of the season, ESU finished 3rd behind McCleary's 4th place finish in 26:24 and Reid Bauersfeld's 13th in 26:44.

ESU stepped it up to finish 3rd in the MIAA Cross Country Championships held at Pittsburg State, with the University of Central Missouri and Northwest Missouri finishing ahead of the Hornets. Shane Osterhaus ran in the Hornet number one slot to finish 8th in 26:09 with McCleary 17th in 26:32.

The NCAA regional meet was hosted by Hillsdale, Michigan. The Hornets were 6th over the 10K course in the race won by MIAA member, Northwest Missouri State. Osterhaus again led the way running 33:19 and Reid Bauersfeld 28th in 33:29.

1999

Jonathon Campbell emerged as the Hornet number one runner, finishing 13th in the season opener at Wichita State as the team finished 4th. Campbell led the team to 3rd place at the Fort Hays Invite with a 5th place finish in 35:03 over the 10K course. Osterhaus stepped up to lead the Hornets to 4th in the home meet, with a 13th place finish, followed two seconds later by Campbell in 14th. The MIAA meet was won by the University of Central Missouri, with the Hornets 6th. Again, Osterhaus led the way with a 20th place finish in 26:29 and Campbell in 31st at 27:10. At the NCAA Regionals in Joplin, Missouri, the men finished 16th of 22 teams, led by the 47th place finish of Meyer in 24:24.

2000

The 2000 cross country season started at the Mule Run with a 3rd place team finish. Campbell led the men with an 8th place finish, followed by Andrew Bird in 12th, and Jason Dolan in 30th. Campbell again led the ESU effort to a 2nd place team finish at the ESU Invite, finishing 2nd in 25:52, followed by Bird in 18th. ESU won the Baker Invite, scoring a low 28 points behind the winning effort of Campbell in 25:46, Bird in 4th, Dolan in 8th, and Luke Rodina in 10th. ESU finished 5th in the MIAA behind champion Missouri Southern. Campbell raced to a 4th in 25:46 and Bird a 20th place finish in 26:35.

The NCAA Regional Championships were hosted by Texas A & M Commerce. Abilene Christian won the 10K race with a low 19 points. The Hornets placed 6th, led by Campbell in 16th at 34.40. The next five finishers for the Hornets were all freshmen with Bird (25:13), Rodina (36:29), Dolan (36:55), Michael Wienandt (38:13), and Chris Bell (38:55). For the first time since Jermaine Mitchell in 1996, the Hornets qualified a competitor for the NCAA Cross Country Championships. The national meet was hosted by Cal Poly Pomona at Prado Park, Chino, California. Campbell finished the 10K course in 33:20 for a 53rd place finish at the national meet.

2001

Jonathon Campbell returned off his previous season of competing in the national meet. He helped lead ESU to the Swede Invitational title and a 3rd place finish at the ESU Invitational. At the home meet, Campbell finished 9th in 25:57, followed by Jared Dittmer in 13th. Andrew Bird was the top ESU finisher in three of the last four meets for ESU. His mark of 25:35 was the fastest time for the Hornets over 8 kilometers this season. Antony Kariuki was the top finisher for ESU at the Border States Championships. Jared Dittmer was the top finisher for ESU at the KSU Invitational and the SBU Invitational.

The team finished 5th in the MIAA and took 6th in the South Central Regional, again led by Campbell in 20th, running 32:28 for the 10K course. Roger Edmonds ran number two for the Hornets in 26th place at the regional meet.

2002

The 2002 men's cross country team won three meets in 2002: the Southwest Baptist Invitational, the ESU Invitational, and the Border States Championships. The men finished 4th in the MIAA meet and 5th in the NCAA South Central Regional.

Bird led the way at the MIAA Championships with a 12th place finish in 25:35, followed by Antony Kariuki's 16th in 25:45. Bird led the way at the NCAA South Central Regional garnering a 14th place and national qualifying finish in 33:21, followed by Kariuki in 16th in 33:28 over the 10K distance, with the team finishing 5th. At the 2002 NCAA Cross Country Championships held in Ashland, Ohio, Bird represented the Hornets by placing 68th.

2003

ESU started the 2003 cross country season with a win at the Southwest Baptist Invitational. Bird led the way in 6th at 26:42, followed in 7th by Tyler Applegate, freshman Eric Wellman in 8th, Sam Farleigh in 9th, and Ryan Weston 10th. Only 27 seconds separated runners 1-5. The Woody Greeno Invitational at Lincoln, Nebraska saw the Hornets place 9th of 24 teams, led by Bird in 13th at 26:06, Weston in 19th in 26:22, and Applegate 36th in 26:55. On the familiar turf of Jones Park, the Hornets won the ESU Invitational, taking the measure of 10 teams with Bird 3rd in 25:27, Weston 6th in 26:05, Wellman 14th in 26:56, and Sam Fairleigh 15th in 26:58.

The harriers placed 5th in the MIAA behind the 3rd of Bird in 25:57, 19th of Weston in 27:11, and Wellman in 31st at 27:41. Competing in the South Central Regional, ESU placed 10 of 16 scoring teams with the following placers: Bird in 10th in 31:21, Sam Fairleigh in 50th in 33:40, Ryan Weston in 59th in 33:58, Luke Rodina in 61st in 34:00, and Eric Wellman in 70th in 34:35. The men struggled to overcome the mid-season injuries to Wellman and Applegate. Bird, running in his last collegiate cross country race, came up two spots and 2 seconds short of qualifying for nationals for the second year in a row. Only two individual qualifying spots were available and Bird finished in 10th place, running 31:21 for the 10K.

2004

The 2004 men's cross country season began with a successful opener at Southwest Baptist. The men placed 2nd as a team, led by the 6th place finish of Tyler Applegate in 26:40, followed by Chris Stearns 7th in 26:47, Weston 8th in 26:49, and Emporia High product Brock Ternes 16th in his first collegiate race. Freshman Stearn's 32nd place finish helped the men to a 9th place Woody Greeno at Nebraska finish. Stearn continued to lead the Hornets at the ESU Invitational to a 2nd place finish behind Mid-America Nazarene, as he placed 5th in 25:33. Stearns ran with two Chinese Symbol tattoos on his left arm that meant "courage" and "strength." Weston, Applegate, and Garrett Frank were 9-10-11 with Wellman 13th, Stephens 15th, and Ternes 18th. Applegate led the way at the Border Invite finishing 19th of 273 runners with a team positioning of 5th.

ESU had one of their highest finishes ever in the MIAA, finishing 2nd behind Central Missouri. It was only the second time that ESU finished as high as 2nd in the MIAA and it was their best finish since 1994. In a tight finish, ESU edged Truman by 3 points and Missouri Southern by 5. Ryan Weston ran 5th in 26:50 to lead the team, followed by Stearns in 6th in 26:54, Applegate in 13th, Stephens in 24th, and Ternes in 35th. The regional meet saw Applegate place 12th to lead the team to a 5th place finish. He was an agonizing 3 seconds away from qualifying for nationals.

2005

After finishing 2nd in the MIAA Championships the previous year, tying the highest team finish ever, the hopes were high heading into 2005 cross country season. However, the 2005 men's team was very low in numbers and when several injuries hit early in the year, Coach Harris decided to redshirt the entire team. Therefore, there are no official results for the 2005 cross country season.

No Team

One of the lowlights in Emporia State Cross Country history occurred in the 2005 season. For the first time since 1954, the Hornets did not field a team. The 2005 men's team was very low in numbers and when several injuries hit early in the year, Coach Harris decided to redshirt the entire team.

2006

After a year's hiatus, the men's team returned to action in 2006. Skyler Delmott led the Hornets to a season opening Maple Leaf Invitational team victory with his 6th place finish over the 5K Course in 16:06. Marcus Summers placed 9th in 16:26, and Ternes 12th in 16:33. The Hornets finished 2nd at the Woody Greeno and the ESU Invitational meets. Their MIAA finish of 8th place was the lowest finish for ESU since joining the MIAA. Delmott was the top finisher at 19th in 25:36. ESU placed 10th at the South Central Regional meet with Delmott in 28th place, leading the Hornets as he did in every race in 2006.

2007

The 2007 cross country season was highlighted by a team win at the ESU Invitational, with three Hornets placing in the top 10. Delmott led the way with a win in 25:20, followed by a 4th for Brock Ternes in 25:53, a 5th by Summers in 26:01 and a 9th by Wellman in 26:29. At the Missouri Southern Stampede, Delmott (25:29) led the Hornets, followed by Ternes (25:41). ESU finished 5th in the Border States, and 4th in the MIAA led by Skyler Delmott in 7th and Ternes in 13th. Delmott had the highest finish by a Hornet since Ryan Weston finished 5th in 2004. Sloane Kern was 19th and was the top freshman finisher and earned the inaugural MIAA Cross Country Freshman of the Year Award. Wellman was 22nd for ESU in his final MIAA Cross Country Championships, competing during the season with a pin in his foot due to a broken bone.

The team finished 5th at the South Central Regional with Delmott leading the way in 31:38 for 10K. Ternes 27th in 30:30, Kern 28th in 32:32, Stephens 46th in 33:14, and Wellman 51st in 33:24 closed out the scoring.

2008

The 2008 men's cross country team was led by Skyler Delmott, who led the way in every meet that season. The season was highlighted by wins at the Maple Leaf Invitational and the ESU Invitational. ESU put five in the top 11 to take the home the title at Baker. Sklyer Delmott led the way in 2nd with a 25:09, Adam McGovern was 5th, Will Hohmeier 7th, Kern 9th, and Asher Delmott (Skyler's younger brother) 11th. ESU placed 4th in the Mule Run and 6th in the Greeno Invitational in Lincoln, Nebraska.

At the ESU Invite, the men won for the second straight year, paced by the second of Skyler Delmott. Skyler Delmott also placed in the top 10 to earn All-MIAA honors for Emporia State at the MIAA Cross Country Championships in Warrensburg, Missouri. The Hornet men placed 7th in the team standings. Skyler Delmott had a career-best 5th place finish for the ESU men. At the South Central Regional, Skyler Delmott again led the way in 11th in 31:56 for 10K, as the team finished in 8th place.

2009

The 2009 team started the season with a 4th place team finish at the Bob Timmons meet hosted by the University of Kansas. Skyler Delmott led the way with a 13th place finish in 19:55 followed by McGovern in 18th at 20:21, then Asher Delmott in 20th at 20:25.

Skyler Delmott led the team to a 10th place finish at Woody Greeno hosted by the University of Nebraska placing 30th in 26:06 for 8K. McGovern and Hohmeier followed in 49th and 53rd. Skyler Delmott again led the men at the Tabor College Invitational in Hillsboro by placing 2nd in 25:26 to lead four Hornet men in the top 10. McGovern placed 6th, followed by Asher Delmott in 8th, and William Hohmeier in 9th.

At the ESU Invitational, McGovern was the top collegiate finisher, just in front of teammate Skyler Delmott to pace the Hornets to their third straight ESU Invitational team championship. Will Hohmeier was the third ESU runner in the top 10 with an 8th place finish, followed by Asher Delmott in 12th, Dillon Cowling in 23rd, and Andrew Wayman in 33rd. ESU picked up a 2nd place team finish at Tabor College with McGovern leading the Hornets with a 3rd in 25:36, led by Skyler Delmott's 2nd place in 24:26. The Emporia State men finished 2nd at the Ollie Isom Invitational in El Dorado. For the second straight meet, McGovern led the ESU men, placing 5th overall with a time of 15:29 on the 5K course. Hohmeier finished 9th with a time of 15:40, while Skyler Delmott was 11th at 15:47 for ESU.

ESU finished 5th in the MIAA, hosted by Emporia State at Jones Park, with a 12th from Hohmeier in 25:42 (first time Hohmeier had finished in the number one position), as Skyler Delmott (25:51) was battling a hamstring injury. Asher Delmott finished 17th and ESU added a 51st from Ryan Hahn in 27:09. ESU finished the season at the South Central Regional with a 7th place team finish, only seven points out of 5th. Skyler Delmott finished 30th in 32:25, Hohmeier was 32nd in 32:47, and Asher Delmott was 39th in 33:15.

2010

The 2010 men's team started off the season with the always challenging Woody Greeno Invite in Nebraska with a 5th place finish. ESU finished 2nd at the Tabor College Invitational with Asher Delmott leading the men's team with a 6th place finish overall. Hohmeier also placed in the top 10 in 9th place. ESU's top eight finishers all placed in the top 25 overall. ESU placed four runners among the top 30 to finish 2nd to Missouri S & T at the ESU Invite. Hohmeier paced the Hornets with a 15th place finish overall with a time of 25:49 on the 8-kilometer course. Asher Delmott, who had been ESU's top finisher in the first three meets of the year, finished in 21st and Jacob Bull placed 26th overall for the Hornets.

The MIAA Championships were held at Fort Hays with the men finishing 8th. The ESU placers were: 16th- Hohmeier 25:20, 24th- Delmott 25:42, 34th- Bull 25:59, 44th- Marcus Portofee 26:13, and 45th-

Wayman in 26:15. The South Central Regional saw the men finish 11th behind the 26th place finish of Hohmeier in 33:12 and the 44th place finish of Asher Delmott in 33:48.

2011

The Hornet men finished 14th of 28 teams at the Woody Greeno Nebraska Invitational to start the 2011 season. Asher Delmott placed 40th overall out of over 300 runners to lead the Hornet men. ESU's second through sixth runners were all within 45 seconds of each other. The 2011 cross country team won the Tabor Invitational with Asher Delmott 2nd with a 26:41 over the 8K course. Morgan Riggs, Ryan Hahn, Marcus Portofee, and Jacob Bull finished 8th, 10th, 11th, and 12th, respectively.

David Harris Era

David Harris coached four cross country All-Americans: Jermaine Mitchell, Andrew LaRouche, Kadri Kelve, and Jonel Rossbach in his 19 years as ESU head cross country coach. The 1994 women's team won the first and only MIAA cross country title in ESU cross country history. The 1993 cross country team qualified for the national meet and placed 12th.

Asher Delmott led the Hornet men to another team title at the Haskell Invitational. Delmott finished 5th as all five of ESU's scorers placed in the top 25. Bull joined Delmott in the top 10, running 26:55 to place 9th. Riggs was 11th at 27:14, Hahn ran 27:38 to place 19th, and Trey Brokaw was 22nd with a time of 27:51 to round out the ESU scorers.

The Emporia State Invitational was challenging, as the Hornet Harriers placed 6th at the ESU meet led by Delmott in 26:24 in 19th, Riggs 32nd, Bull 35th, and Hahn 39th, all within 32 seconds of each other.

Riggs led the effort at the MIAA Championships finishing 27th, running 25:22 with Asher Delmott 30th in 25:32 and Bull in 37th at 25:49. Delmott took back the number one spot for the Hornets at South Central, placing 47th, with Bull in 52nd while as a team, the Hornets finished in 10th place.

2012

ESU started off the 2012 season with a 10th place finish at Wichita State, with Riggs leading the Hornets over 6K in 19:53 to place 18th. Riggs ran 27:18.17 to finish 76th in a field of 175 runners at the Missouri Southern Stampede as Emporia State was 13th in the team competition. Freshman Daniel Claassen and transfer David Keach both placed in the top 100 for Emporia State.

The Emporia State Invitational had entries from 25 schools and more than 350 runners, with the Emporia

Eric Wellman: Coach

Eric Wellman competed in cross country/track and field for ESU from 2003-2008. He was the men's high point scorer at the 2006 MIAA indoor meet, winning the mile, 3000 meters, and anchoring the MIAA record-setting distance medley relay team. Wellman won five MIAA championships as an athlete. Wellman served two prior years as an assistant with the program.

State men placing 5th, as Riggs led the Hornet men with a 25th place finish. He covered the 8-kilometer

course in 26:52 to lead five Hornets in the top 50. Claassen ran 27:01 to place 28th as the second Emporia State runner. Brian Mosier was 35th and Jacob Bull 49th to round out the scoring for the Hornets. The men won the Tabor Invite led by Riggs, who ran 26:35.53 over the 8-kilometer course, with Keach placing 6th. The men placed 10th of 10 teams at the MIAA meet with Riggs leading the effort, placing 52nd with a 27:20, Portofee 59th in 27:34, and Bull 60th with a 27:54. ESU did not enter any men at the regional meet, electing to run only Taylor Stueve on the women's side.

2013

The Emporia State men started the 2013 cross country season off on a positive note as they won the team title in the College Division of the J.K. Gold Classic hosted by Wichita State in Augusta, Kansas. ESU placed four runners in the top 10 in their division. Jacob Bull led the Hornet men with a 3rd place finish in a time of 19:35 over the 6000-meter course. He was joined in the top 10 by Riggs in 5th place, Keach in 7th and Claassen in 9th place for the Hornets. ESU placed 10th out of 18 teams in the college division of the Woody Greeno Invitational in Lincoln, Nebraska. Bull led the Hornet men with a 15th place showing.

The Emporia State men placed 4th at the ESU Cross Country Invitational at Jones Park. Bull led the Hornet men with a 9th place finish running 26:55 over the 8-kilometer course to pace three Hornet men in the top 25 out of 171 men's finishers. Riggs placed 16th at 27:21.99 while Keach ran 27:43.85 to finish 23rd overall. ESU finished 4th at the Rim Rock Classic hosted by KU. For the fourth straight meet, Bull led the Hornets placing 3rd in the college division with a time of 26:07 on the eight kilometer course. Riggs also registered a top 10 finish, running a 26:45 to place 10th overall with Keach close behind at 26:54 to place 11th.

The men struggled at the MIAA meet and finished 9th with Bull once again the top finisher for the Hornets. He covered the 10-kilometer course in 33:45 to finish 40th overall, with Riggs and Keach placing 58th and 70th, respectively. The Emporia State men placed 18th out of 23 teams at the NCAA Division II Central Region Championships in Sioux Falls, South Dakota. Bull was again the top finisher for the Hornets, covering the 10-kilometer course in 33:45 to finish 65th overall.

2014

The 2014 men's cross country team struggled to find consistent success. The squad started off the season with a 7th place finish at Wichita State. James Bowlin led the Emporia State men, running 20:26 over the 6 kilometers to place 20th and was followed closely by Claassen at 20:28 to place 21st. Freshman Thomas LaRoche ran 20:43 to finish 31st, Riggs was 32nd in 20:45 and Cody Miller was 42nd at 21:06 to round out the top five scorers for the Hornet men.

The men were 8th at the ESU Invite, and LaRoche was the top finisher for the Hornet men in 34th place. The Hornet men ran in a tight pack with Riggs placing 39th, Claassen 43rd, and Alex Skinner in 47th with just 27 seconds separating the four of them.

Competing at the Kansas University Rim Rock Invitational, ESU finished 6th in the College Division led by LaRoche in 27:25 for 8K. LaRoche again led the Hornets at the Southwest Baptist Bearcat Invite in Bolivar, Missouri, as he finished 32nd in 28:03.

The MIAA meet was one of major disappointment for ESU, as the Hornets struggled, finishing 9th of 9 teams. ESU's top individual finish was the 52nd place of Cody Miller in 27:06. ESU elected not to compete as a men's team at the South Central Regional.

2015

The ESU men started the 2015 season with a dual against Newman University and an individual victory with Daniel Claassen running 26:18 over the 8K course. However, the next six runners were all from Newman as they defeated ESU 20-41. The following weekend saw the harriers finish 12th in the college division of the Woody Greeno/Husker Invitational in Lincoln, Nebraska. Claassen again ran as number one man for ESU, finishing 64th overall.

ESU hosted their only home cross country meet of the year on the traditional last Friday of September, running in Jones Park in northwest Emporia. A field of 10 teams lined up. Claassen again led the Hornets as he had done in the previous two meets and placed 3rd individually with the team garnering 2nd place honors. Brian Mosier was 9th and Brian Newkirk 13th to aid the Hornet score. Aaron Taylor and Thomas LaRoche finished in 18th and 19th as the Hornets put all five scorers in the top 20.

The Emporia State cross country teams got their first look at the course for the 2015 MIAA Championships when they competed at the Fort Hays State Tiger Open at the Sand Plum Nature Trail in Victoria. ESU finished 17th with Thomas LaRoche taking his turn as the top placer for the Hornet men, running 26:51 to place 97th over 8K. Two weeks after the Tiger Open, the Hornets journeyed to Hays for the MIAA Cross Country Championships. The Hornets finished 9th in the nine-team conference field led by Daniel Claassen in 46th place, followed closely by Brian Newkirk in 47th and Thomas LaRoche in 54th.

The Emporia State men's team ended their season in Joplin, Missouri, competing in the NCAA Central Regional Cross Country Championships. Brian Mosier was the top finisher for the Hornet men, placing 101st in a time of 33:14 over the 10-kilometer course, as ESU placed 21st as a team.

Epilogue

Emporia State University has established a legendary tradition in cross country. ESU started cross country competition at the national level with a 5th place finish at the 1946 National Intercollegiate Championships. In 1954, the program re-started and has continued for the last 63 years. The Hornet harriers claimed NAIA cross country championships in 1958, 1959, 1961, and 1962 and a NCAA small college national championship in 1963. They finished as the national runner-up in 1963 and again in 1964. Ireland Sloan in 1962 and John Camien in 1963 and 1964 won individual NAIA National Championships. Eighteen athletes have earned cross country All-American honors in Emporia State University history.

The Hornets have competed in both NCAA and NAIA national competitions and in several different conferences in their 60 plus years of competition. Cross country has been successful at Emporia State through the determined efforts of athletes and coaches. Fellow Kansas schools Pittsburg State and Fort Hays State have been formidable and worthy opponents with highly respected programs that have challenged Emporia State. Emporia State has risen to the challenge to become one of the legendary cross country programs in the history of collegiate track and field.

Women's Cross Country

1980

For the first time ever, Emporia State fielded a women's cross country team in the same year that the NAIA added women's championships in cross country and track. The first year women's team would thus compete in the NAIA instead of the AIAW. However, unlike most first year squads, the Lady Hornets were very competitive. Freshmen Lesha Wood and Nancy Gray and sophomores Cindy Edgerton, Patty Herrick, and Kay Hoffman were consistent scorers during the season. They opened the season placing 4th among 15 teams at the Wichita Gold Classic, then won the Bethany Invitational, the Marymount Invitational, and the Kearney Invitational. The Lady Hornets won the initial Central States League title. The Lady Hornets' 33 points bettered Fort Hays' 2nd place total of 41. Lesha Wood finished 3rd in 18:27 behind the winner Janet Wilson of Pittsburg, who won in 18:14. Other Hornets scoring on the 3-mile course were Cindy Edgerton 4th in 18:55, Kay Hoffman 8th in 19:21, Patti Herrick 9th in 19:22, and Nancy Gray 10th in 19:29. E-State's sixth and seventh runners, Cheryl Phares and Caron Swaney, finished 11th and 22nd, respectively, among 25 runners, before competing in the District 10 Championships. The Lady Hornet harriers continued a successful season by placing 2nd behind Fort Hays in the District 10 meet. Wood led the effort in 5th, with Edgerton 9th and Herrick 11th, Hoffman 14th, and Gray 15th.

On a cold 24-degree day with three inches of snow on the ground, the Lady Hornets competed in the first-ever NAIA National Women's Cross Country Championships held in Kenosha, Wisconsin. The Lady Hornets were in the running for the national title and finished 2nd behind the host team, Wisconsin Parkside. Wood finished 4th in the NAIA meet, running 18:39 to earn All-America honors and pace E-State. Herrick (19:44) and Edgerton (19:48) placed 26th and 27th, respectively, to just miss All-

1980 Women's XC Team: National Runner-Up

The 1980 women's cross country team was the first in ESU history. The Lady Hornet harriers placed 2nd behind Fort Hays in the NAIA District 10 meet and finished 2nd behind Wisconsin Parkside in the very first NAIA Women's National Cross Country Championships.

Bill Tidwell: Coach

Bill Tidwell was the coach of the first women's cross country team in ESU history, starting in 1980. Tidwell coached the ESU women's teams through the 1983 cross country season. One of the top distance middle distance runners in the 1950s, he was a four-time NAIA champion in the 880 and the mile. He has been inducted into numerous athletic Halls of Fame including the NAIA Hall of Fame and the Kansas Sports Hall of Fame. His amazing 800 record of 1:47.61, set in 1955, still stands over 60 years later.

47

American recognition. Kay Hoffman (19:52), Nancy Gray (20:07), Cheryl Phares, (20:17), and Carol Swaney (21:27) rounded out the national scoring for E-State's strong 1980 cross country team.

1981

The 1981 Lady Hornets picked up where they left off in 1980, with only Kay Hoffman gone from the NAIA runner-up squad. Lesha Wood again paced the E-State women through the season. The women placed consistently throughout the season, placing in the top five as a team in every meet. The Lady Hornets won the Pittsburg State dual with Wood winning in a personal best 17:37 over the 3-mile course. Herrick ran 2nd, Gray 4th, and Edgerton 5th. ESU won at the Fort Hays State Invitational and then dominated at the Southwest triangular sweeping the top six places. They claimed their second consecutive CSIC Championship, sweeping the top three places with Wood, Herrick and Edgerton, leading a 1-2-3 sweep. ESU dominated the meet with Wood winning in 18:12 for three miles. Herrick finished runner-up only 13 seconds behind Herrick. Edgerton was another five seconds back to give ESU a sweep of the top three places. Gray was 6th in 19:23, Garhan 8th in 19:31. As a note of interest, Fort Hays State which fielded one of the better teams in the area, did not participate.

Lesha Wood: All-American

Lesha Wood was a standout in track and cross country from 1980-1984. She earned seven All-American honors and led three cross country teams to top 10 national finishes. Her highest national finish on the track was a 2nd place runner-up in the 1500 meters.

Wood again led the Lady Hornets, winning the district individual title, as the team captured the crown and qualified for the NAIA national meet that was held in Kenosha, Wisconsin. ESU nosed out Fort Hays State by a score of 27-29, as only two schools fielded full teams. Wood won in 17:52, with Edgerton 30 seconds back. Herrick recorded a 5th in 18:33, Gray 8th in 19:05, and Kelly McCammon was 9th in 19:28.

Wood ended the season with a 10th place finish in the NAIA Championships to again earn All-American honors in cross country, while Emporia State took 4th as a team in the national meet. Cindy Edgerton just missed earning All-American honors for the second consecutive year, finishing 26th in the field of 105 runners. Rounding out the outstanding squad were Herrick (30th), Gray (42nd), sophomore transfer Susan Garhan (43rd), freshman McCammon (62nd), and Phares (67th).

1982

The 1982 Lady Hornet cross country team remained one of the top teams in the Midwest and the NAIA. The Lady Hornets were ranked in the NAIA top 15 all season, and moved up as high as 7th during the latter part of the season. Also ranked high in the NAIA polls were the Fort Hays Lady Tigers. Lesha Wood won the ESU Invitational running 18:14 over the 3-mile course. However, no team scores were kept, as ESU was the only team with a complete squad. ESU won the Marymount Invitational led by the 18:47 3-mile time from Wood. Similar results occurred at the Pitt State Invitational and the Southwestern

Invitational as Wood and the Lady Hornets won. As women's cross country was in the early stages of development, the entries in each meet were very limited with only two to three teams competing. Because of a lack of teams, the CSIC meet was not held. Hays just nipped E-State (27-30) for the District 10 title after the Hornets had won the three regular season meetings between the two squads. Wood won the individual District 10 title in 17:45. Only two complete teams competed in the District 10 Championships. However, the Lady Hornets regained the upper hand at the NAIA nationals, defeating Fort Hays while placing 12th in the field. Wood was 8th in the field of 215 runners in 18:28 over the 5000-meter course to become an NAIA All-American in cross country for the third consecutive year. Scoring at the national meet was provided by Herrick in 44th in 19:46, Edgerton 68th in 19:46, McCammon 107th in 21:36, Dena Wymore 117th in 21:48, Suzanne Graziano 127th in 22:20, and Garhan 129th in 22:35.

1983

The 1983 women's cross country team was a mixture of the old and the new. Several of the outstanding performers who had been running since the beginning of the program had graduated, but veterans Kelly McCammon, Lesha Wood, Susie Garhan, and Nancy Gray combined with freshmen Joni Dutton and Peggy Teichgraeber once again provided Emporia State with a strong women's team. For the first time since the program began, Wood was not leading the Lady Hornet harriers. McCammon had matured into a strong cross country runner and she finished as E-State's top performer in every meet throughout the season. ESU won the home invitational with a perfect score of 15, defeating seven teams, although there were only two complete teams competing. ESU won again the next week at the Bethany Invitational, with McCammon winning in 18:13 over 3 miles. ESU would finish 2nd in the next two meets, the Marymount and Barton County Invitationals.

McCammon added a victory, running 18:14 in the CSIC Invitational, as ESU captured the team title and defeated two other teams. Wood in 4th and Dutton in 10th added to the winning effort. McCammon added a runner-up finish in the district meet with Wood and Dutton placing 4th and 10th, respectively, and these three high finishes helped lead the Lady Hornets to the district team title. The Emporia State women ended the season with a 21st place finish out of the 27 teams competing in the NAIA Championships. McCammon finished 39th as ESU's top finisher, running 19:12 over the hilly course in Kenosha, Wisconsin.

Coach Bill Tidwell Era

The five year tenure of Coach Bill Tidwell was characterized by starting one of the most successful women's cross country teams in the NAIA. He coached the very first women's cross country team at ESU and led the women to a national runner-up finish and two other finishes in the top 10 at nationals. Tidwell coached one All-American in cross country and nine All-Americans in track and field.

1984

The E-State women's cross country team opened its fifth season of competition in the fall of 1984 with a new coach. Former E-State cross country and track standout Mark Stanbrough took over the coaching duties. Stanbrough returned to his alma mater eager to continue the tradition of excellence that the young ESU women's cross country program had achieved in its first four years.

Although the 1984 women's team was small in numbers, the quality of the returning runners was outstanding. Returning for her senior year was Kelly McCammon, who had won the CSIC title while leading the team in every meet the previous season. Sophomores Joni Dutton, an All-District performer, and Peggy Teichgraeber also returned in 1984.

McCammon picked up a victory in the home ESU Invitational ran on the ESU campus course with an outstanding performance of 16:57 over the 3 miles.

Mark Stanbrough: Coach

Mark Stanbrough was the second coach in ESU women's cross country history. Stanbrough had competed in cross country and track and field for the Hornets from 1977 under Coach Phil Delevan. After graduation, he was an ESU graduate assistant in track and cross country, then taught and coached at Glasco High School for two years. He obtained his Ph.D. in exercise physiology from the University of Oregon. While in Oregon, Stanbrough competed for Athletes In Action and the Oregon Track Club.

Her winning time was 1:29 faster than the 2nd place finisher. Dutton and McCammon were slowed by injuries during the year, as Dutton was forced to drop out and McCammon was unable to compete at the Swede Invitational, but McCammon came back the following week to win the Marymount Invitational in 18:16. She would win again at Barton County the next week, with Dutton returning for a 5th place finish.

At the CSIC meet hosted by Fort Hays, McCammon won the individual title for the second consecutive year. She turned in a 17:52 clocking over the 3-mile course despite strong winds over the rolling hills to remain undefeated over the season against small college competition. Dutton finished 2nd in 19:29 and Teichgraeber 4th in 20:42. None of the four conference schools finished with a complete team and since four schools had to take part in the meet to make it an official CSIC championship race, there were no official team scores.

ESU hosted the 1984 Distinct 10 meet on the ESU campus home course. The winning team would earn a berth in the NAIA National Championships in Kenosha, Wisconsin. The Lady Hornets had been running with only three runners the majority of the year, but Stanbrough wanted to post a team score on their home course. Sprinter Charlotte Purcell and high Jumper Shari Larimer were added to the team for the meet. Stanbrough informed his athletes since they had not been a team during the year, they were a team for this meet only and they would have to qualify to nationals as individuals. The Lady Hornets, with Purcell and Larimer stepping up for the team, competed well on the home course and ESU won the meet. McCammon took the win in 18:18 over the 3-mile course, moving up one spot from her District 10 finish the year before. Dutton added a 6th in 19:54, Teichgraeber a 9th in 20:43, and Purcell an amazing 11th in 21:11. Larimer completed the ESU scoring to finish 24th in 24:43.

Although the Hornets won the District meet and the single team-qualifying berth to the national meet, Stanbrough held to his pre-meet statement that the Hornets would have to qualify for nationals as individuals. That put McCammon in the national meet, but 6th place finisher Dutton was left out by one spot. With the Lady Hornets declining the team berth, Kansas Wesleyan accepted the berth and competed in the national meet two weeks later.

As the lone representative at the 1984 NAIA National Cross Country Championships in Kenosha, Wisconsin, McCammon capped an amazing season with a 16th place finish to become a cross country All-American to go with her two track and field All-American honors earned during the 1984 indoor season.

Kelly McCammon: All-American

Kelly McCammon competed in track and cross country from 1982-1986. She was the NAIA national champion in the indoor mile in 1986. She earned six All-American honors, including one in cross country. Her finest hour as a Lady Hornet came when she set two new school records in the 1500 and 3000 meters in the span of one hour, finishing 2nd and 4th, respectively, in those events at the 1986 National Outdoor Track and Field Championships. These records still stand over 30 years later.

1985

With the addition of several highly recruited freshmen and newcomers, the Lady Hornets entered the 1985 season eager to compete. Two of the freshmen made an immediate impact at the season-opening Wichita State University Gold Classic held at Cessna Activities Center Golf Course. Gloria Bates and Susan Stine finished 3rd and 4th in a tight battle to be the number one ESU runner, finishing one second apart in 19:15 and 19:16 for the 5K distance on a windy day. Junior Amy Potter, a transfer from Allen County, ran third for the Lady Hornets in 20:25, finishing slightly over a minute ahead of her mother, Marilyn, who ran for Allen County Community College. Freshman Jean Kolarik ran in the fourth slot, as the newcomers led the Lady Hornets to the team title over Wichita State.

Bates would remain as the number one runner the following week at Kansas, with Stine as number two, as the women finished 5th as a team behind Nebraska, Kansas, and Drake. Nebraska put up a perfect 15 points as they took places 1-5. The young Lady Hornets started to gain confidence with a win at the Marymount College Invitational. With 11 teams represented, ESU dominated to win by 42 points. Bates, Stine and Potter went 1, 2, and 3. Teresa Pattison ran 4th and Stephanie Dryer completed the team scoring.

Emporia State hosted its only collegiate meet of the year and finished 5th as a team at the Emporia Invitational. A strong Kansas State team led by the NCAA national caliber trio of Jacque Struckoff, Alysun Deckert, and Anne Stadler led the Wildcats to a perfect 15 points. Stine finished 7th and stepped up to the number one team spot that she would seldom relinquish for the next two years. Bates and Potter held the 2-3 spots although Potter's mother (running for Allen County) did cut the gap down to under a minute from her daughter.

The Swede Invitational hosted by Bethany College and held at the Lindsborg golf course was an outstanding meet, and drew the top NAIA teams from Kansas and Nebraska as well as some junior colleges. Stine placed 3rd, going under 19 minutes for the first time over a 3-mile course, followed by fellow freshman Gloria Bates also going under 19 minutes. ESU finished 3rd in the 20-team competition.

Seeking excellent competition, the Lady Hornets journeyed to Fayetteville, Arkansas, home of the University of Arkansas and one of the great traditions in college cross country. ESU found the stiff competition they were looking for, finishing 7th behind Nebraska, Oklahoma State, Arkansas, Colorado, and Oklahoma. Stine led the team over the 5K course in 18:28 with Bates back in 18:49 and Potter breaking 20 minutes, running 19:37.

The CSIC conference meet was held in Kearney, Nebraska with freshman Stine winning in 18:46, Potter was 3rd in 19:36 and Bates 6th in 19:49. Pattison ran 20:09 for 11th and Ann Stoll finished the scoring in 17th. Despite the win from Stine, the Hornets lost by six points to Kearney and would also finish 3 points behind Fort Hays for a 3rd place conference finish. The 1985 District 10 meet was held at Fort Hays with the top team qualifying for the single berth at nationals. The year before the women's team had won the District 10 meet despite running only three cross country runners all year and adding a sprinter and high jumper for the district meet. However, the competition had improved significantly the following year. Fort Hays edged out Emporia by the score of 32-36. Stine won in 18:34 for the second consecutive week, building on her CSIC championship and defeating Mary Griebel of Fort Hays by six seconds. Griebel would later transfer to ESU and become a key part to future teams. Stine's teammate, Gloria Bates, finished 3rd in 18:51, and Potter followed in 7th, Pattison in 11th, and Kolarik in 15th.

The Hornet trio of Stine, Bates, and Potter represented ESU as individuals at the 1985 NAIA National Cross Country Championships the following week in Kenosha, Wisconsin and gained valuable experience and a foundation for upcoming success at future nationals. Stine finished 58th, Bates 123rd, and Potter 132nd. Counting the seven men ESU qualified as a team, plus the three individual women, the contingent was the largest ESU representation in school history. With 22 of the 24 members of the 1985 ESU men's and women's cross country teams new to the program, the cross country future looked bright as the ESU cross country program was determined to maintain and establish ESU history.

1986

After a much-improved season the year before, the 1986 Lady Hornets were starting to focus on team success. Led by senior Amy Potter at the season-opening Wichita State University Gold Classic, ESU placed five runners in the top 10 to win the competition. Potter had put in the off-season work to improve dramatically and she wasted no time in displaying her improved skills. Potter's time of 18:26 was two minutes faster than the time she ran on the same course a year earlier. The Lady Hornets finished 2nd behind K-State and were also edged out the following week by six points by Kansas University at the KU Invitational. Potter again led the women, running 18:27, followed by Susan Stine, Gloria Bates, and Trudy Searcy. Searcy ran at Barton County Community College and transferred to ESU, not intending to compete at ESU. However, when Coach Stanbrough found out she was on campus, he quickly visited the young runner and persuaded her to walk on and continue her career. She later set the ESU school record at 10,000 meters and became an All-American.

The 1986 Emporia Invitational was a display of ESU dominance, with the Lady Hornets racking up a perfect score of 15 points led by Stine, Potter, and Searcy. One of the toughest competitions of the 1986 season occurred at the Swede Invitational at Bethany. The Air Force Academy out of Colorado Springs edged out Emporia 60 to 68. Sophomore Stine led the Hornets, her 3rd place time of 17:53 cutting almost a minute off her previous best time.

Stine continued her winning ways at the Pittsburg State Invite. The sophomore from Pleasanton ran 17:30 to PR again. Teammates Potter (17:50) and Bates (17:51) also got PRs as the Hornets placed five runners in the top 10 to win by 47 points.

The Lady Hornets were rolling and full of confidence as they returned to Pittsburg State for the CSIC championships. Stine (17:43) lead a 2-3-4-5 Emporia finish to a low score of 21 points over the 3-mile course. Potter, (3rd in 17:55), Bates (4th in 18:09), Dutton (5th in 18:22), and Searcy (7th in 18:26) gave ESU five in the top seven for a dominating victory.

The women entered the District 10 meet looking to get a win and a berth to the national meet. Placing five runners in the top eight in another dominating performance, they finished with only 19 points, far ahead of defending champion Fort Hays' total of 68 points. Senior Potter led a 1-2-3 sweep, winning the 5K race in 18:03, Stine was 2nd in 18:12 and Bates was 3rd in 18:44, Dutton was 6th at 19:04, and Searcy was 8th at 19:12. All five ESU runners were under the course record.

The Lady Hornets capped an impressive season by finishing 2nd to host Wisconsin-Parkside at the 1986 NAIA National Cross Country Championships in Kenosha, Wisconsin. Parkside finished with 121 points and ESU totaled 151 points. Thirty-five teams and 289 individuals finished the competition. ESU's leading runners again were Stine and Potter, who both earned All-America honors. This was the only season in women's school history that ESU has had more than one cross country All-American. Stine, the CSIC champion, finished 14th in 18:15 while Potter, the District 10 champion, was 16th in 18:17. Bates finished 40th in 18:45. It was a dramatic improvement for the three who ran at nationals the year before. Stine moved up 44 places and ran over two minutes faster. Potter moved up an amazing 116 places and ran 3 minutes

faster, Bates moved up 83 spots and ran over 2 minutes faster. Searcy had a tremendous race, finishing 48th in 18:48. Dutton had fought a stress fracture the first half of the season but battled back to finish 74th in 19:15. Jean Kolarik was 179th in 20:33 and Peggy Teichgraeber 214th in 21:00 completed the team results.

1987

The Lady Hornets entered the 1987 season fresh off a 2nd place finish in the national meet. Despite losing cross country All-American Potter and outdoor track All-American Trudy Searcy to graduation, five letter winners returned, so there was considerable excitement for the 1987 season. Susan Stine returned for her junior year and was joined by Mary Griebel, a junior transfer from Fort Hays, and Cindy Blakeley, a senior transfer who was 36th in the 1986 NAIA National Cross Country Championships. Blakeley had started her career at the University of Kansas, then transferred to Ottawa University.

The promising season started at the Wichita Gold Classic with a 2nd place team finish with newcomer Blakeley immediately making an impact by leading the Hornets over the 3-mile course with a 6th place finish in 18:09. Griebel finished 8th in 18:08 and Stine, battling an injury, placed 14th in 18:56. The Hornets competed as the only non-NCAA school in the seven-team Jayhawk Invitational cross country meet at Rim Rock Farm. The Lady Hornets, paced by Blakeley's win, totaled just 38 points to best Kansas University with 54 points on their home course. The meet was especially satisfying for Blakeley. She competed on the 5000-meter course as a freshman for the University of Kansas, before transferring to Ottawa University, and then to ESU. The Lawrence Journal World newspaper did a preview on the meet and never mentioned the Lady Hornets as a contender, only have to have ESU emerge victorious, shocking the NCAA DI schools. Blakeley threw in a powerful surge with slightly more than a mile remaining to take the lead and cruise to a 15 second victory 18:11 over the 5K course. Griebel finished 3rd in 18:42 and Stine followed in 4th in 18:50. Michelle Tyrrell, a freshman from Osawatomie, finished 10th in 19:19.

Fresh off the victory over KU, the Hornets moved up to the number one ranking in the NAIA Cross Country National Rankings. The Hornets demonstrated why they

---

Amy Potter: All-American

Amy Potter competed for the Hornets from 1985-1987. Her 16th place finish at the 1986 NAIA National Cross Country Championships helped the Lady Hornets to a NAIA runner-up finish. Potter won the 1986 District 10 cross country title.

Lady Hornets Shock Jayhawks

The Lawrence Journal World newspaper did a preview on the 1987 Jayhawk Cross Country Invitational meet and never mentioned the Lady Hornets as a team contender. After all, there were seven teams competing and ESU was the only non-NCAA school. However, the Lady Hornets paced by Cindy Blakeley's win totaled just 38 points to best Kansas University with 54 points on their home course. The win was especially satisfying for Blakeley, as she ran for KU as a freshman before late transferring to Emporia State.

From left to right: Blakeley, Stine, and Griebel lead the Emporia Invitational

54

were ranked so highly at the ESU Invitational by placing the top 5 scoring runners among the top 10 for an impressive 20-point total. Blakeley and teammates Stine and Greibel ran together through the first mile of the 5000-meter course. Blakeley began to pull away in the second mile, opening a 30-yard lead over her teammates and went on to win in 18:56 with Stine 2nd in 19:19. Griebel finished 4th in 19:37. Tyrrell add a 7th place and Jennifer Strader a 10th to round out the scoring.

The Hornets continued to crush the fields with five among the top 10 again in the 20-team field at the Swede Invitational in Lindsborg. Blakeley, bothered by illness, still managed a 2nd place finish in 17:23 over the 3-mile course. Stine followed in 4th (17:44), and Griebel in 5th (17:57), as ESU totaled just 25 points with a whopping 59-point victory over Fort Hays. The Hornets traveled to the SW Missouri Invitational and placed 3rd in the 6-team field. The Hornets did not run Blakeley, and Tyrrell led the way with a 10th place finish. ESU continued an impressive season by placing five runners in the top 11 to again beat the University of Kansas at the Pittsburg State Invitational. The Lady Hornets, competing without an injured Stine, totaled 30 points to the Jayhawks 40. Blakeley led ESU with a 2nd place finish 18:04, Griebel was 5th in 18:34, and Tyrrell 7th in 19:04. Blakeley also won the Southwestern Invitational as the Hornets finished 2nd in holding some runners out.

The Lady Hornets had proven themselves worthy of being a national contender over the course of the 1987 season. The District 10 championships posed a challenge for the Hornets. Although they had no returners back to defend their championship from the previous year, the Hornets were still the overwhelming favorite to win the meet. Stine was fighting injuries and was held out of the meet, Potter and Dutton had graduated, Bates got married, and Searcy transferred to pursue a career in physical therapy. However, the Hornets had a dominating runner in Blakeley. Blakeley had finished the previous year's district meet in 4th place behind three Lady Hornets when she ran for Ottawa. In a competitive, supporting team environment at ESU, Blakeley prospered to finish 1st or 2nd in 6 meets. The Lady Hornets ran the 1987 conference meet on their familiar home campus course. For the first two miles, Blakeley ran even with Kearney State's outstanding runner Donna Spickelmeier, who had finished 5th in the NAIA National Cross Country meet the previous year. The two built a lead of approximately 100 yards on the rest of the field. After climbing Highland Hill, they entered a wooded area out of the view of the spectators. When

Cindy Blakeley: All-American
Cindy Blakeley earned All-American honors in cross country in 1987, finishing 9th in the NAIA national meet. She was the national runner-up in the 1988 indoor mile, setting a new ESU record. Blakeley went on to have a long career competing as an active runner, winning numerous national masters awards.

the two emerged some 45 seconds later, Blakeley had a 25-yard lead and later explained, "As soon as I got over the top of the big hill, I didn't slow down. I just kept accelerating into the little hills. A lot of people don't pay much attention to those little hills. But when you've run the course enough times, you know you have to."

Griebel fell early but recovered to finish 5th, Tyrrell was 8th, Strader 11th, and Kolarik 16th. Despite the conference win, the women realized they still had work to do to qualify for nationals. It would take a top-two team finish to qualify. The Hornets totaled 35 points to edge host Pittsburg State with 40 points. Blakeley again established her dominance, taking the lead at the mile mark and running solo to the victory with a 33-second winning margin in 18:19. Tyrrell continued her tremendous rookie season, teaming with Griebel to run 2nd and 3rd behind Blakeley until the last half-mile of the race, with Tyrrell finishing 4th and Griebel 5th.

The Lady Hornets finished 11th in the NAIA National Cross Country meet with Blakeley topping off a fantastic season by finishing in 9th place to earn All-American recognition. Her time on the hilly 5000-meter course in 17:52 was her first time under 18 minutes for 5K. Tyrrell finished 79th in 19:13, Griebel was 81st in 19:13, Strader 118th in 19:43, Kolarik in 138th in 19:56. After finishing 14th in the meet a year earlier, an injured Stine finished 163rd, running through pain to help her team.

1988

The Lady Hornets entered the 1988 season with only two of the their top seven runners returning off of the District 10 and CSIC championship team that finished 11th at the NAIA Nationals the previous year. With four-time All-American Susan Stine red-shirting, a relatively inexperienced cross country team carried the ESU banner in 1988. ESU started the season with a 2nd place tie at Wichita State led by Strader in 8th, Gretchen Bohm in 9th, and Tyrrell in 10th. A highlight of the season included a 2nd place team finish at the ESU Invitational behind Kansas State. Strader led the Hornets in 10th, followed by Bohm and Tyrrell in 12th and 13th, respectively. Bohm took over as the number one runner at the Swede Invite to lead the team to a 3rd place finish. Bohm had arrived in Emporia as an accomplished sprinter from Cheney High School. Stanbrough convinced her to run cross country and she was a back-of-the pack runner her first year. However, her tremendous work ethic led to gradual improvement every year and eventually she worked her way up to be the team front runner and leader.

Strader contended for the number one runner in leading a Lady Hornet 4-5-6 finish at the Southwest Missouri State triangular, as the women were edged out of the team title by a single point by Memphis State. ESU picked up another 2nd place finish, their fifth of the season, at the Southwestern Invite with Bohm running 19:21 in 7th place.

The Lady Hornets were unable to defend their conference and district titles they had won the previous two years. They finished 4th in the CSIC meet, only three points out of 2nd, behind the 7, 8, 9 finishes of Strader, Bohm, and Tyrell. The women were 3rd in the District 10 meet, led by Strader's 10th place finish. The 1988 season was an up and down season with ESU finishing out of the top two district spots for the first time in history and with no national qualifiers for the first time in Stanbrough's five years of coaching at Emporia State.

1989

The 1989 cross country season began at the Wichita State Gold Classic. The women, competing against three NCAA schools, captured a 2nd place finish. A very balanced attack helped ESU sneak up on some quality teams in the women's race. Junior Michelle Tyrrell paced the squad with an 8th place finish in 19:54, with Bohm and freshman Katie Wheeler following in 9th and 10th.

ESU finished 4th at the Kansas University Invitational behind Michigan, Kansas, and Eastern Michigan. Pacing the Lady Hornets were Tyrrell and Bohm, who finished 15th and 20th, in times of 20:10 and 20:33. Freshman Michelle Hebb finished strong as ESU's third runner. The times were affected by prior heavy rains making the course soft and adding to the challenges of the demanding hills of the KU Rim

Rock course. Bohm led the ESU women to a meet championship at the Baker University Invitational, finishing in 3rd with a 19:31 for the 5K course. Freshmen Wheeler and Hebb finished in 5th and 6th place. The Lady Hornets won again at the ESU home meet, scoring 21 to Hutchinson's 36 points. Senior Bohm held back to help Hebb and Wheeler along for part the race. At the midway point of the 3-mile race, Bohm took a 20-yard lead over Hebb and Wheeler that she held to the finish.

The Emporia State women rolled to a convincing win at the Swede Invitational by using great team running. Five ESU women finished in the top 20, with Hebb finishing 2nd in 19:42, only one second off the winning pace. Bohm placed 4th and Wheeler 7th. Confusion reigned in the race, as the leader took a wrong turn at 2.5 miles and the entire field followed, necessitating officials to improvise in directing the runners to a modified finished line. The course ran by the competitors ended up an unknown distance, but farther than the originally planned 3 miles.

ESU competed in a unique and enjoyable relay race in 1989 called the *Ekedin* relay, hosted by Allen County Community College. The Japanese term originally referred to a stagecoach that transmitted communication by stages. The concept involves runners racing relay legs of various lengths, a nice break from traditional cross country racing. The women raced legs of 1 mile-2 mile-1 mile with the men racing miles of 1-2-3-2-1. Northeastern Oklahoma captured the women's title while ESU decided to split their teams into two equal teams and finished 2nd and 4th in the 8-team field. The ESU freshmen-only team of Andria Van Durme, Hebb, and Wheeler came out on top of the veteran team of Stine, Bohm and Laura May.

The Hornets had traditionally used the Southwestern Invitational as a final tune-up before the conference and districts meets. Racing on a flat and fast course, the Hornets had fared well in the past and 1989 would be no exception as they won easily with 17 points. Bohm raced to a 18:50 PR win and was followed by Hebb and Wheeler. The Lady Hornets established themselves as the District 10 favorites by going 1-2-3 and placing six runners in the top 10, scoring a very low 17 points.

With the defection of some schools to the NCAA Division II, the CSIC conference disbanded, so ESU did not compete at a conference meet and instead turned the focus to the District 10 Championships. With a trip to nationals on the line, the Hornets needed to win the meet to advance and were returning to the course where they had won a title at the Baker Invitational earlier in the year. ESU won their sixth district title in the last nine years by placing 1-2-3 with freshman Hebb the individual district champion, followed by freshmen Wheeler and senior Bohm, who was bothered with a knee injury and unable to train all week. Tyrrell also earned All-District honors by placing 8th.

The 1989 NAIA National Cross Country Championships were held on a cold, windy day in Kenosha, Wisconsin. ESU ran well as a pack with a time gap of 35 seconds for runners 1-5. Entering the meet unranked, they finished with a 14th place showing. It was the sixth time in nine years since the program started in 1981 that they had finished in the top 15 teams. Wheeler finished 99th (19:39) and led the Lady Hornets to become the fourth number one runner of the year. Hebb finished 117th (21:51), Bohm was 119th (19:53), Tyrell was 133rd (20:01), and Stine finished 157th (20:14). Four-time All-American Susan Stine finished her outstanding cross country career after injury plagued junior and senior campaigns.

1990

With several returning runners, the 1990 cross country season was a successful one. ESU finished 2nd at the Pittsburg Invitational on the flat, fast course of Four Oaks Golf Course with Hebb 2nd in 19:10,

Jennifer Mullen (a transfer from Johnson County) 4th in 19:20, Tyrrell 7th in 19:37 and Ingrid Frazier 10th in 19:43. Fast times continued at the traditionally fast course at Missouri Southern as ESU finished 3rd behind DI schools Missouri and Arkansas with Frazier 7th in 18:13.

ESU defended their home turf with an Emporia Invitational win over a seven-team field with a perfect score of 15 points, with Frazier, Hebb, Mullen, Tyrrell, Fitzgerald and Brenda Bina all finishing in the top six. Frazier and Hebb went 1-2, both breaking 19 minutes, running 18:52 and 18:59. The traditionally strong Barton County women defeated the ESU women at the Swede Invitational on a hot and windy day that slowed times down. Mullen led the women, finishing 4th in 19:47 over the 3-mile course, followed by Hebb and Frazier in 5th and 8th.

ESU journeyed to Kenosha, Wisconsin in the middle of the season to run on the National Cross Country Course and prepare for the national competition later in the year and finished 3rd in the competition, only two points out of 2nd in the meet won by Loyola University, Illinois. Mullen ran 18:47 on the tough course to finish 3rd, just 11 seconds off the winning time, followed by Hebb in 11th in 19:22. The Southwestern Invitational only had two completes teams and ESU posted a perfect 15 points on Oklahoma Christian. Mullen (18:53), Frazier and Hebb went 1-2-3, and Wheeler, Fitgzerald and Tyrell went 6-7-8.

For the second year in a row, ESU did not compete in a conference meet and the team championship focus was on the District 10 meet. Just as they had done a week earlier at Southwestern, the Lady Hornets pulled off a 1-2-3 finish in the same order as Mullen (18:23), Hebb (18:42) and Frazier (18:47) dominated the District 10 meet. Tyrrell added an 8th, Bina, Fitzgerald and Kerri Stine finished 13, 14, and 15, giving the Lady Hornets eight of the top 15 runners and a convincing win over Fort Hays.

The Lady Hornets returned to Kenosha, Wisconsin for the second time in the 1990 season, this time to compete in the National Championships. The women notched a top 10 finish, finishing 9th led by the All-American run of Mullen in finishing 20th in 18:28. Frazier was 41st in 18:57, Hebb 49th in 19:10, Tyrrell 130th in 20:06, Wheeler 161st in 20:28, Brenda Bina in 194th, and Maureen Fitzgerald in 225th, completed the scoring in the field of 327 runners.

1991

The Lady Hornets came into the 1991 season off a top 10 national finish (9th place) at the NAIA Cross Country Championships the previous year. Since the inception of women's cross country, ESU had dominated the NAIA District 10, winning seven of the 10 titles. Jennifer Mullen and Ingrid Frazier returned to lead the Lady Hornets. In the previous cross country season, Mullen was 20th in the 1990 National Cross Country Championships and Frazier had finished 41st and they returned as the top two district runners. Both had earned All-American honors in track.

The season started at the Pittsburg State Invitational with a 3rd place team finish led by Mullen and Frazier. They led the way again at the Missouri Southern Stampede finishing 6th in the 18 team field.

Both clocked fast times in 18:14 and 18:24, respectively. The Lady Hornets continued to improve finishing 2nd in the Emporia Invitational and winning the Swede Invitational hosted by Bethany College. Mullen won both races, with Frazier 3rd at Emporia and Hebb finishing 3rd at the Swede Invitational. Hebb, battling injuries would be a significant factor in the District 10 and National meets.

Coach Stanbrough's philosophy that facing better teams would make only make you better, led to the Hornets competing the next two meets at the Oklahoma State Cowboy Jamboree and the Arkansas Invitational. The competition was top-notch and the Hornets posted quality times with the top three of Mullen, Hebb and Frazier breaking 20 minutes on both 5K courses.

The Lady Hornets won their second team title of the 1991 season at the Southwestern Invitational as Mullen defeated the NAIA National Marathon Champion, Peggy Murphy of Oklahoma

Christian, to lead the women to a victory. At the District 10 meet held in Emporia in sub-zero wind chill temperatures, the Lady Hornets could not defend their team title, finishing 2nd to Fort Hays (36-44), but still qualified for nationals. Mullen and Hebb repeated their 1-2 finish of the previous year, marking the third year in a row the Lady Hornets went 1-2 at District 10 and the 7th time in the last 8 years the Lady Hornets had won the individual title.

The traditionally strong women's team finished their last year in the NAIA with a top 20 finish. ESU turned the tables on Fort Hays at the national meet, finishing 16th to Fort Hays' 22nd place finish. The Lady Hornets used their 1-2-3 punch to put three women in the top 100. Mullen struggled in the mud and could not duplicate her 20th place national finish from the previous year, but still led the Hornets with a 58th place finish (19:36). Hebb (66th/19:46) Frazier (87th/19:58), Michelle Bradbury (169th/21:01), and Fitzgerald (256th) completed the scoring.

The 1991 cross country season signaled the end of the NAIA era for Emporia State University Athletics.

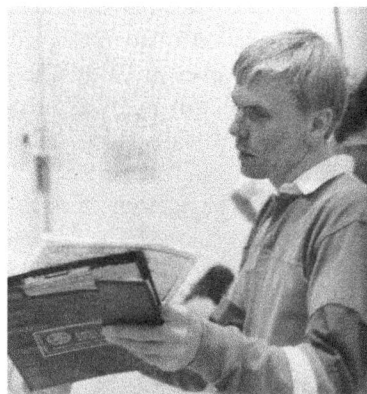

1992

1992 was a year of great change for ESU. The Coach Stanbrough era had ended and David Harris was hired to lead the ESU program. After 35 years of competing in the NAIA, ESU moved to the NCAA Division II level of competition and joined the Mid-America Intercollegiate Athletics Association.

The Lady Hornets started off the 1992 season at the Wichita State University Invitational with Hebb, the only Hornet harrier returning from the previous season, finishing in 16th place and the women finishing 6th as a team. Hebb followed up at the Southern Stampede with a 9th place finish in 18:49, as the Lady Hornets finished 5th in the six-team field. Hebb continued to lead the women at the ESU Invitational as she led early on the home course and eventually finished 3rd, 13 seconds behind winner Catherine Kilat of Butler County, who won in 20:37. ESU's Lisa Ball was 9th in 21:30.

For the first time, ESU competed in the MIAA Cross Country Championships and finished 4th. Hebb again led the Hornets placing 8th individually in 18:56. Angela Cathcart had joined the women's team less than a month before the conference meet and broke the 20-minute barrier for the first time in her career, finishing in 11th with Laura Edwards in 30th.

At the Great Lakes Regional Cross Country meet the women finished 14th out of 18 teams led by Hebb's 17th place finish covering the 5K in 19:12. Following Hebb was Cathcart (59th), Ball (74th), Edwards (76th) and Jamie Lynn (115th).

David Harris: Coach

David Harris was hired to lead the ESU program. Harris came to ESU after a seven year stint as an assistant coach at the University of Nebraska, where he coached 31 All-American and three Olympians. Harris received his bachelors' degree in physical education/social science and a master's degree in athletic administration from Northeast Missouri State University. While competing for the Bulldogs, he was a four-year letterman in cross country and track and field.

The original Missouri Intercollegiate Athletic Association was formed in 1912. When Emporia State started MIAA play in 1992, the conference changed its name to Mid-America Intercollegiate Athletics Association. The conference has had two national championship teams in cross country with the Southwest Missouri men's team winning in 1971 and 1984.

1993

Coach Harris entered his second year of leading the Lady Hornet cross country program in 1993 with the cross country season starting at the Wichita Gold Classic. Angela Cathcart picked up where she had left off the previous season leading the Lady Hornets with an individual win and a team win over the 3-mile course in 19:05. Annette Posgai emerged as the team leader at the Missouri Southern Stampede with a 19:28 for a 16th place finish in the very tough and challenging field. Posgai would again lead the Hornets to a 2nd place team finish at the Emporia State Invitational. Posgai and Cathcart ran 5th and 6th in the MIAA, running 18:57 and 18:59, with the Hornets taking 3rd as a team. The Lady Hornets competed in the Great Lakes Regional and completed the season with a 10th place finish. Cathcart was the top ESU finisher in 12th running 18:46.

1994

Newcomer Katarina Nilsson led the team throughout the 1994 season and she started by placing 2nd at the Jayhawk Invite, leading the team to a 3rd place team finish. Nilsson's time of 19:58 over the 5K course was 8 seconds off the winning time. Freshman Cheri Hopkins finished 10th in 20:09. At the Woody Greeno Invitational in Lincoln, Nebraska, the Lady Hornets won the college division, edging out Doane by 3 points. Nilsson again set the pace finishing 4th overall with a time of 19:02 over 5K. Sophomore Annette Karjala (formerly Posgai) stepped up and took 8th in 19:31, followed by Cathcart in 9th at 19:39.

First MIAA Champions

1994 marked the first MIAA cross country championship ESU had ever hosted and they took advantage of the home course to win the first MIAA title in any sport in school history. In an amazing display of team running with a time-gap between runners 1-5 of only 15 seconds, the Hornets placed five runners in the top 15 to win.

The Hornets traveled to Minneapolis, Minnesota to compete in the Minnesota Invitational. The team, ranked 14th at the time in the NCAA DII poll, took 2nd place among the 29 DII schools competing. Nilsson finished 11th, posting a 18:25 5K PR. Cathcart finished in 28th place, running 18:53.

ESU returned home, and running on the familiar training territory of Jones Park, won the ESU Invitational, edging Fort Hays State 44-47. Nilsson was 4th in 19:02, with Posgai close behind in 5th at 19:09.

The 1994 MIAA cross country meet was hosted by Emporia State and held at Jones Park. This marked the first MIAA cross country championships ESU had ever hosted and they took advantage of the opportunity to win their first MIAA title in any sport in school history. The ESU title ended Pittsburg State's three-year run. The Hornets placed five runners among the top 15 finishers with an amazing 15-second split between runners 1-5 to edge Northwest Missouri State, 41-50. PSU finished 3rd with 70 points. Surprisingly, the Hornets' number one runner the majority of the year, Nilsson, was battling illness and dropped to fourth runner. The Hornets scored with Mary Daniel, a transfer from Allen County (19:12) in 4th, Billi Jo Ross, a Butler County transfer in 5th (19:18), Karjala in 7th in

Division II was officially christened in 1973 when NCAA members voted to establish three divisions for athletics competition. Before then, NCAA schools were classified as either "university" or "college" to distinguish between the larger and smaller athletics programs, but the three-division structure adopted in 1973 gave NCAA members a more varied menu for which to classify their programs.

(19:21), Nilsson (19:27) in 10th, and Cathcart (19:39) in 15th.

To qualify out of the Great Lakes Regional for the National Cross Country Championships, the Lady Hornets needed a win to advance to nationals. The Lady Hornets came into the Great Lakes Regional meet ranked 7th in the nation but were defeated by unranked Ashland, 64-95, who claimed the single berth to nationals. The 2nd place finish at the NCAA regionals marked the Lady Hornets' highest finish ever in NCAA regional competition. Daniels led the Lady Hornet effort in 11th place in 19:52 over 5000 meters, with Nilsson 13th in 19:58 and Cathcart 18th in 20:12

1995

The 1995 cross country team finished 3rd in the Maple Leaf Invitational at Baldwin City, led by Jessica Oberg in 12:03 for two miles. Cathcart was 8th in 12:12 and Ross 9th in 12:15.

The Hornets picked up a win at the Missouri Southern Stampede, led by Jessica Oberg, who placed 2nd in 18:50 for 5K. ESU had five finishers in the top 10. Cathcart was 3rd, Posgai 4th, Daniel 7th, and Ross 9th. Although the team started the race slow, they gradually moved up throughout the course of the race to finish with 25 points and beat host Missouri Southern, who was 2nd with 37 points.

Competing at the Cavalier Cup in Johnson County, the Lady Hornets finished 2nd led by Oberg in 19:10 and Ross 4th in 19:12. The Lady Hornets were 2nd at the ESU Invite, as Karjala finished 2nd in 19:07, Daniel 5th in 19:19, Ross 8th in 19:29, Cathcart 7th in 19:40, and Page 10th in 20:02. ESU also finished 2nd at the Southwestern Invite led by Daniel in 5th and Oberg in 6th, followed by Cathcart in 7th. At the Minnesota Invitational, ESU placed 9th. Cathcart led the way with a 21st place finish in 18:55; Ross was 40th in 19:11.

The Lady Hornets were contenders for the MIAA championships but were unable to defend their title from the previous year and finished 2nd to Northwest Missouri. Ross led the Hornets at conference with a 5th place finish in 18:07, with Daniel 12th in 18:24, and Karjala 13th in 18:30. The Hornets finished 5th in the Great Lakes Regional. Ross led the effort with a 21st in 19:11, Karjala 29th in 19:17, Daniel 35th in 19:25, and Oberg 37th in 19:38.

1996

Lacey Robison led the women's team to a 3rd place finish to open the 1996 cross country season at the Maple Leaf Invitational hosted by Baker University. Robison completed the 2-mile course in 12:07 for an 8th place finish. The following week, the Lady Hornets were 3rd at the Jayhawk Invite led by Adrienne Johnson's 31st place finish in 18:33 and the 37th place of Karjala in 18:46. Jessica Oberg clocked 19:00 to finish 44th. ESU won the next two meets, the Emporia Invite and the SMU Invitational. In the Emporia meet, ESU won behind the 3rd place finish of Robison (19:30), 4th of Karjala, 5th of Oberg, 7th of Johnson, and the 8th of Magali Schneider. Schneider had tremendous versatility, as she was an All-American in the 60-meter dash in track and field.

ESU took a team 2nd at the Central Missouri State Invite led by Johnson in 12th at 19:54 and the 13th of Schneider. Johnson and Schneider again led the team finishing in 4th and 5th in 19:02 and 19:03, respectively, at the Oklahoma Baptist Invitational. Tara Frey was 8th in 19:30 as ESU finished 2nd behind the host school, Oklahoma Baptist.

ESU finished 4th at the MIAA meet held in Kirksville, Missouri and again Johnson led the way finishing 12th in 19:39, with Oberg and Schneider both running under 20 minutes and finishing in 18th and 19th. At the Great Lakes Regional meet held at Central Missouri, Johnson led the team to a 9th place finish, covering the course in 19:21.

1997

The ESU women opened the 1997 cross country season with a 2nd place finish at the Wichita Gold Classic. Tara Hudspeth led the way with a 10th place finish in 12:10 over the 2-mile course, followed by Johnson in 11th at 12:18 and Aileen Murphy 12th in 12:29.

ESU added a 9th place overall team finish and 1st among small college teams at the SMU Invite. Johnson in 36th place at 19:37 led the way. Running at home in the Emporia Invitational, the Lady Hornets were victorious defeating Fort Hays State by eight points. Leading the Hornet victory was Tara Hudspeth in 4th place (17:56), with Johnson (5th) Eileen Murphy, (6th), Deandra Doubrava (7th), and Casey Wilson (13th).

The winning streak stretched to two meets in a row, as the Lady Hornet won the Ollie Isom Invitational, placing five runners in the top eight. Johnson and Hudspeth went 1-2 overall with Murphy 4th, Jalayne Gerber 6th, and Wilson 8th.

ESU continued the season with a 5th place finish at the MIAA championships. Hudspeth was 13th in 19:48, Johnson 14th in 19:56, and Doubrava 3rd in 20:58. The Great Lakes Regional saw Johnson finish in 22nd with 18:59 and Hudspeth in 39th with a 19:47 as the top ESU runners. ESU only fielded three runners in the regional competition.

1998

ESU started the 1998 season at the WSU Gold Classic finishing 5th behind four NCAA DI schools. Tara Hudspeth led ESU with a 23rd place finish in 19:57. Hudspeth again led the Hornets in a tough KU field with a 65th place finish. The Lady Hornets won the Cavalier Cup at Johnson County behind the 1-2 finish of Hudspeth and Johnson. Lacey Kirkaldie, Sara Ferguson, and Alicia Rooman all added top 10 finishes.

Hudspeth and Johnson went 3-4 at the ESU Invitational with ESU finishing 2nd behind Northwest Missouri State. Emporia State raced to a 5th place MIAA finish at Pittsburg State with Hudspeth in 9th with a 19:02, Johnson in 16th at 19:52 and Robin Childers running 19:58 for 18th. At the NCAA regional championships held in Hillsdale, Michigan, the women were 9th with Hudspeth leading the way in 29th in 23:41 for the 6000-meter race.

1999

Tara Hudspeth led ESU in every meet, finishing 6th at the WSU Gold Classic, and winning at Fort Hays and the ESU Invitational. ESU captured the Fort Hays Invite with Hudspeth's winning time at 23:53 for

6K, followed by Michelle Hein in 24:43, and Johnson 5th in 24:53. Hudspeth's winning time of 18:38 at the ESU Invitational led ESU to the team title, with Johnson following in 8th. Hudspeth again led ESU at the MIAA as she became the first ESU woman to win an MIAA cross country individual championship. Hudspeth ran the 6K in 21:59. Johnson and Ferguson followed in 13th and 14th, with the women finishing 4th as a team.

Hudspeth topped off an outstanding season with an 8th place finish at the Great Lakes Regional in Joplin running 22:35 for 6K. Hein was the second runner as the women's team finished in 12th place.

2000

Just she had the previous year, Hudspeth led the Lady Hornets in every meet through the 2000 cross country regular season. The Hornets started the season with a 2nd place finish behind the University of Central Missouri at the UCM Invite over the 2-mile distance. Hudspeth went 12:02 and was followed by ESU places of 7, 8, 9 with Janice Yingst, Robin Childers and Sara Ferguson. The Lady Hornets won at the Southern Methodist University meet with Hudspeth finishing 10th. At the ESU Invite, Fort Hays edged ESU 62-66. Hudspeth again led the way with a 2nd place finish in 18:52 and Childers in 3rd at 19:10. ESU captured the Baker Wildcat Invite with Hudspeth, Childers, and Ferguson going 2, 3, and 6. ESU finished 4th in a tight MIAA championship race, which saw Truman win by one point over Central Missouri. Hudspeth and Childers went 3-4, running 22:33 and 22:41, with Ferguson in 15th. Central Missouri rebounded to win the Regional with ESU finishing 4th as a team, with Childers 8th and Hudspeth 9th running 24:41 and 24:43 over the 4K course.

2001

Tiffany Lytle led the ESU 2001 cross country team in the season opening Mule Run with a 9th place finish over 2 miles in 12:27 as the team finished 3rd. The team won the Swede Invitational with a low score of 27 points. Lytle again led the team in 2nd. Other finishers for the Hornets were Childers in 4th, Stacy Marshall in 6th, Covington in 7th, Liddick in 8th, and Visser in 10th. At the ESU Invite, the freshman Kristin Loyd cracked the top 10 in 7th, with Lytle in 10th. Marshall in 12th and Liddick in 18th finished in the top 20 as ESU placed 3rd. The MIAA championships were held at Jones Park in Emporia. The host team placed 6th in the eight-team field. Sophomore Lytle finished 27th in 41st, Loyd Covington 48th, and Liddick 41st. ESU only started three runners at the NCAA South Central Regional hosted by Missouri Southern with Crystal Covington the top performer in 69th as the Lady Hornets failed to field a team score.

2002

The Hornet women started the 2002 season with a 2nd place finish at the Southwest Baptist Invitational led by Kristin Loyd. Loyd also led the women at the K-State Invitational, as they finished 4th as a team. Kadri Kelve ran in her first meet of the season at the home ESU Invitational and emerged victorious with a mark of 17:46 that shattered the old record for the course as the Lady Hornets finished 2nd. Childers placed 4th in 19:15, followed by Kristen Loyd in 7th with a 19:29. Amy Zeller had the top finish as the women placed 10th in the Border State Invite. Kelve returned to win the MIAA Championship with meet record time of 21:30 over the 6-kilometer course and lead the women to a 6th place team finish. Kelve became only the second ESU runner to win the MIAA cross country individual title. Lytle ran in the number two spot with a 28th place finish.

Kelve was outstanding to finish her senior season, placing 8th in the South Central Regional and running to an All-American honor with a 13th place NCAA finish. She became the first woman in ESU history to earn NCAA DII All-American honors in cross country and the first cross country All-American since Jennifer Mullen earned NAIA honors 12 years earlier. Kelve's 13th place showing was the best by an Emporia State woman since Cindy Blakely placed 9th at the 1987 NAIA Championships.

2003

The 2003 women's cross country squad opened with Megan Haight finishing 4th over the Southwest Baptist 5K course, but ESU was unable to field a complete team in the scoring. Haight again led the way at the Woody Greeno Invitational in Lincoln, Nebraska with a 20th place

Kadri Kelve: All-American
Kadri Kelve became the first female runner from Emporia State to earn All-American honors in cross country at the NCAA DII level. Kelve placed 13th at the 2002 championships and also captured two MIAA cross country titles. Kelve capped off her outstanding career by winning the 3000-meter steeplechase at the 2003 NCAA DII National Track and Field Outdoor Championships in meet record time.

finish, running 23:32 over 6K, as the team placed 19th. ESU competed in their only home meet of the year and finished 3rd at the ESU Invite, with Haight in 4th at 19:06, and Melissa Visser in 9th at 20:00.

The MIAA Cross Country Championships saw the Lady Hornets finish 8th of 8 teams with Haight and Visser running in their customary one and two slots for the Lady Hornets finishing in 20th (24:06) and 26th (24:25). The South Central Regional was hosted by Texas A&M Commerce and again the Lady Hornets struggled placing 13th of 18 scoring teams with Visser besting Haight by 9 seconds as they finished in the 35th and 36th place positions.

2004

The 2004 women's cross country season started at Southwest Baptist with Kristen Larson and freshman Krista Fennewald running 5th and 6th in 20:07 and 20:12, respectively for the 5K course. Haight followed in 14th in 20:58, Aniesa Slack 21st in 21:31, and Jonel Rossbach 22nd in 21:33. Larson followed up with ESU's top placing of 38th at the Woody Greeno in Nebraska, running one and a half minutes faster than the previous year on the same course, as the women finished 16th.

Larson continued at the ESU Invitational with the women taking the team title and Larson moving up from finishing 21st the previous year to a 3rd place finish, improving her time by 2 minutes. Larson's vast improvement was partially attributed to solving the anemic problem that she battled the previous season. Fennewald was 4th in 19:08. Fennewald was only in her second year of cross country, as she started running cross country as a senior at Blue Springs, Missouri High School. Rossbach was 7th in 19:46 followed by Haight in 19:59.

At the Border States Invite, the team finished 13th with Larson at 33rd in 19:20 and Fennewald 39th in 19:26. The team moved up in the MIAA to 5th, an improvement from the 8th and last place finish from the previous season. The trio of Larson in 8th (23:46), Fennewald 15th (24:10), and Jonel Rossbach 34th (25:37) led the way. Larson would again lead the team at NCAA Regionals with a 14th place finish.

2005

Kristen Larson picked up the 2005 cross country season with the same success she displayed the previous year. She was 6th in the Baker Invitational, running 12:33, with Robyn Lee 9th in 12:42 over the 2-mile course. Larson ran a PR by over a minute and a half at Nebraska at the Woody Greeno Invite running the 6K Course in 23:01. Having coached as a Nebraska assistant, Coach Harris liked to take his teams to Nebraska to face a large and tough field to run on a fast course at Pioneer Park. The 2005 team finished 13th with Rossbach improving by an amazing two and a half minutes to run 23:54 and place 51st.

Larson led the team to the Emporia Invitational title with a 2nd place finish in 18:30 and followed that up with a 15th place finish at Border States in 18:59, with Rossbach one place and one second behind her for a team 7th place finish. Rossbach led the team at the Ollie Isom Invite, finishing 5th with the team in 3rd.

At the 2005 MIAA Championships at Pittsburg State, Larson was 4th in 22:07, followed by Rossbach in 5th in 22:11. Finishing out the scoring at conference were Robyn Lee, 28 in 23:28, Megan Haight 29th in 23:35, and Betsey Gant 34th in 23:47.

The South Central Regional in Abilene, Texas, saw Rossbach finish 17th over the 6K course with a time of 24:13, with Larson running her last cross country race as a Hornet and finishing 34th in 24:46. ESU fell one runner short of fielding a complete team. Haight finished 60th in 25:49 and Lee finished 74th in 26:45.

2006

Jonel Rossbach continued to make tremendous improvement in 2006. She was the number one team runner in every meet. She finished 3rd at the ESU Invitational in 18:05 with Fennewald 5th in 18:53, as ESU finished 5th as a team. Rossbach captured the MIAA title running 21:28 over 6K. Despite the winning effort by Rossbach, the women could only garner a 6th place finish at the meet. Fennewald at 22:35 and Robyn Lee at 24:19 in 14th and 47th place, respectively, ran in the two and the positions for the Hornets. The Hornets were 12th as a team at the South Central Regional, but Rossbach qualified for nationals by placing 3rd. At the National Cross Country Championships held at West Florida, Rossbach earned All-American honors when she placed 17th in 20:49.

2007

Rossbach continued to shine throughout the 2007 cross country season, picking up a win at the ESU Invite in 16:55 with teammate Kathryn Davison 16th as ESU finished 2nd as a team. Rossbach did not run at the Southern Stampede and ESU's top five women all finished within 16 seconds of each other.

Rossbach successfully defended her MIAA title in 22:06 for the second consecutive year running 22:06 over the 6K course. Coach Harris stated, "It was a great run by Jonel to win her second consecutive MIAA individual championship. She was in control the whole way. She chose not to lead until just past the halfway mark and then pulled away." Rossbach's 1st place finish could not help pull the Hornets out of an 8th place team finish. Kylie Bookout was the second ESU runner and finished in 32nd place.

Rossbach finished 2nd for the second straight year at the South Central Regional in 20:43, followed by Bookout in 61st as the Lady Hornets placed 15th. Rossbach earned All-American honors in cross country, improving upon her 17th at the 2006 NCAA DII cross country championships by placing 4th in the 2007 NCAA Division II Cross Country National Championships in Joplin, Missouri. Rossbach positioned herself 3rd in the race running behind Jessica Pixler of Seattle Pacific and Winrose Karunde from Abilene Christian. With less than 200 meters to go, Tanya Gaurmer of national champion team Adams State moved into 3rd, and Rossbach held on for 4th. The senior from Omaha, Nebraska covered the 6-kilometer course in 20:47.5. Her 4th place finish tied for the best ever by an ESU woman at a national cross country championship meet. She earned All-American honors in indoor and outdoor track as well as cross country for the academic year, becoming just the third ESU women's athlete to pull the trifecta, joining Kadri Kelve in 2002-03 and Lesha

Jonel Rossbach: All-American

Jonel Rossbach earned two All-American honors in cross country and won two consecutive MIAA titles. Her 4th place cross country finish at the 2007 national meet was the best ever by an ESU woman at the NCAA Championships and matched the top finish all-time at a championship meet. ESU Hall of Honor member Lesha Wood placed 4th at the 1980 NAIA National Championships. She also placed 17th at the 2007 NCAA Cross Country Championships.

Rossbach conclude her career as one of the top distance runners in ESU history by winning a national championship at 5000 meters at the 2008 National Outdoor Track Championships, setting a school record.

Wood in 1980-81. Rossbach ran as the top runner for ESU in every meet in 2006 and in 2007.

2008

The 2008 women's team finished 3rd in the Maple Leaf Invitational, 6th in the Mule run, and 14th in the Greeno Invitational. Katie Mona led the women at Woody Greeno, finishing 50th over the 6K in 24:08, followed by Morgan Frehe in 80th at 24:47. Mona won the ESU Invitational in 18:13, leading the team to a 3rd place finish. Frehe and Davison followed Mona to the line in 12th (19:22) and 20th place (19:51).

Mona placed in the top 10 to earn All-MIAA honors for Emporia State at the MIAA Cross Country Championships in Warrensburg, Missouri, placing 9th as the second freshman finisher at the meet. The Hornet women placed 7th in the team standings.

The team was 15th in the South Central Regional with Mona in 28th in 23:01, followed by Tiffany Baum in 65th, and Kathryn Davison in 96th.

2009

The 2009 women's team started the season with a 5th place team finish at the Bob Timmons meet hosted by the University of Kansas. Mona finished 6th to lead the team in 19:35 over the 5K course. Mona led the women with a 21st place finish and an excellent 6K time of 21:56 at the Woody Greeno Invitational in Lincoln, Nebraska, as the team finished 13th in the college division.

The ESU women, running without Mona at the Tabor Invitational, got a 6th place showing from Davison in 19:07 to place 4th as a team. The Lady Hornets had the individual champion at the ESU Invite. With winds blowing between 20 and 40 miles per hour, Mona won her second straight Emporia Invitational individual championship with the 10th fastest time in course history, as the team finished 2nd. Mona's time of 18:17 was nearly 30 seconds ahead of Northwest Missouri's Angel Adams. All five ESU scorers placed in the top 20 for the women. Morgan Frehe ran a personal best of 19:13 to place 7th overall for the Hornets, followed by Davison in 12th, Christy Weller in 15th, and Jaci Willse in 20th.

The women finished 2nd at the Ollie Isom Invitational in El Dorado. Mona was 3rd overall to lead the ESU women with a time of 14:33 over the 4K course. Davison turned in a top-10 performance with a time of 15:17.66 for 8th place.

The Lady Hornets hosted the MIAA meet at Jones Park and placed 8th led by the 24th place finish of Davison in 23:35 over the 6K course. Mona placed 31st (23:48) and Frehe 36th (23:55). The women placed 10th at the South Central Regional, with Mona garnering a 22nd and Davidson a 48th place finish.

2010

The Woody Greeno Invitational in Lincoln, Nebraska was a good early season test for the women's team as they placed 7th in the college division. Katie Mona, coming off a broken foot that caused her to miss all of the 2010 outdoor track and field season, missed the first two meets of the 2010 cross country season. Kathryn Davison was the top placer for the ESU women in 61st overall and 30th in the college division. She was followed by the freshmen trio of Sydney Oltjen in 66th, Courtney Maddux in 74th, and Amy Feldkamp in 79th overall.

The Lady Hornets won the Tabor College Invitational with Mona winning the 5-kilometer women's race by over 10 seconds. She was joined in the top 10 by Feldkamp in 4th, Maddux, in 7th and Oltjen in 9th place. Davison, who had led ESU in the first two meets, suffered from cramps in her calf muscle and finished in 27th place.

ESU finished 3rd at the Graceland Invite and then returned home to run in the largest collegiate cross country meet ever at Jones Park. ESU finished 6th with Mona leading the way with an 18:59 in 13th place. She had won the previous two Emporia Invitationals. Feldkamp was the second runner for ESU finishing in 25th place, followed by Davison, who placed 36th overall.

In the 2010 MIAA Championships the women finished 7th, led by Mona's 13th in 22:23 for the 4K course, Davison was 2nd in 22:57 and Maddux 26th. The women ended the season by placing 12th in the South Central Regionals. Mona finished 19th in 23:18 and Maddux was 40th in 24:06.

2011

The 2011 women's cross country season was highlighted by 2nd place team finishes at Tabor and Haskell. At Tabor, Katie Mona won the individual title, as her time of 18:32 won by nearly a minute. At Haskell, Mona ran 18:29 to finish nearly a full minute in front of Kansas' Devin Wiegers to lead the Hornet women. Courtney Maddux and Amy Feldkamp each had top 20 finishes for ESU. Maddux was 14th with a time of 20:49 while Feldkamp ran 21:01 to place 16th.

Mona had a top 10 finish at the Woody Greeno Invite in Lincoln, Nebraska, running 21:49 for 6K. She placed 10th out of nearly 300 runners in the event and was the second non-Division I runner to cross the line. Courtney Maddux was the second runner for the ESU women, finishing in 152nd place as the Hornets placed 20th out of 25 teams overall.

Katie Mona led the way individually as she won the ESU Invitational for the third time, in 17:30, with the team in 10th. In the MIAA meet, the women placed 8th, with Mona finishing in 8th running 21:44, followed by Feldkamp in 56th, Maddux in 64th, Tiffany Orth in 65th, and Kristen Sponsel in 67th. The women concluded the season by finishing the South Central Regional in 17th place. Katie Mona finished 17th individually at South Central Regional.

David Harris Era

David Harris coached four cross country All-Americans-Jermaine Mitchell, Andrew LaRouche, Kadri Kelve, and Jonel Rossbach in this 19 years as ESU head cross country coach. The 1994 women's team won the first and only MIAA cross country title in ESU cross country history. The 1993 cross country team qualified for the national meet and placed 12th.

2012

The 2012 Lady Hornets had a new look with several freshmen. At the Wichita State Gold Classic, the top six runners for ESU were all freshmen, as the women finished 4th over the 4K distance, led by Taylor Stueve of Las Vegas, Nevada, who placed 20th in 15:42.

The Missouri Southern Stampede saw Stueve place 56th in 19:19 as the women placed 16th. Another freshman led the way at the Emporia State Invitational when Lindsay Cuadra from Derby broke 20 minutes, running 19:57 to place 32nd overall. Stueve was the second Hornet finisher, running 20:04 to place 37th, Susan Welte was 50th, Dominique Staats 51st, and Katie Strickland 74th to round out the women's scoring for Emporia State, with ESU finishing 8th as a team.

Cuadra again led the effort against Tabor as the women prepared for the MIAA meet. The young Lady Hornets, with all seven of their top runners being freshmen, finished 12th in the MIAA. Stueve led the way with a 46th place finish in 24:13 with Dominique Staats 75th in 25:25. ESU entered only one runner at the Regional Championships. Stueve placed 145th overall with a time of 24:52 over the 6-kilometer course in Joplin, Missouri.

2013

As a team, the women won the JK Gold Classic College division to start the 2013 season as they placed four runners in the top 10 in their division. Emily Schoenfeld paced the ESU women in 3rd with a time of 16:05 over 4K and Lindsay Cuadra was 5th overall followed by Taylor Stueve and Susan Welte in 6th and 7th. Cuadra led the Hornets at the Woody Greeno as the women placed 10th as a team. Schoenfeld stepped up again to lead the Hornets at the Rim Rock Classic with a 17th place finish, as the team notched 4th in the college division.

The women placed 7th at the ESU Cross Country Invitational at Jones Park when Cuadra was the top women's finisher for the Hornets in 27th place with a 20:38, followed closely by Schoenfeld in 29th at 20:42. Stueve was the third Emporia State finisher out of 154 total runners with a time of 21:21 to place 43rd overall.

Eric Wellman: Coach
Eric Wellman competed in cross country/track and field for ESU from 2003-2008. He was the men's high point scorer at the 2006 MIAA indoor meet, winning the mile, 3000 meters, and anchoring the MIAA record-setting distance medley relay team. Wellman won five MIAA championships. Wellman served two prior years as an assistant with the program.

ESU failed to place a runner in the top 50 at the MIAA meet hosted by Pittsburg State, as freshman Schoenfeld notched the best effort with a 51st place finish in 23:48 for the 6K distance as the women finished 11th of 11 teams. At the Central Regional in Sioux Falls, South Dakota, ESU only entered four runners and therefore did not have a team score. Schoenfeld ran 23:25 to finish 95th over the 6-kilometer course for the women.

2014

The Emporia State women's cross country team placed 5th at the JK Gold Classic in Augusta, hosted by Wichita State. Emily Schoenfeld paced the ESU women with a 25th place finish to kick off the 2014 cross country season.

The ESU women placed 11th of 12 teams at the Rim Rock Invite led by Schoenfeld in 23:19 over 6K for 35th place and Mercy Perez in 76th. Schoenfeld again led the Hornets at the Southwest Baptist Bearcat Invite in Bolivar, Missouri with a top 10 finish in 8th, as the Hornets finished 4th, their highest team place of the year.

Schoenfeld finished 4th overall in 15:07 over the 4-kilometer course to lead the Emporia State women. Perez was 15th in 16:16, Taylor Stueve placed 19th at 16:32, Brooke Fisher was 27th in 16:51, and Kayla Lansing was 39th in 17:17.91 to round out the top five placers for Emporia State.

The team finished 8th at the home invite as Schoenfeld finished in 7th place overall to highlight the action for the Emporia State cross country teams at the ESU Invite. Following Schoenfeld the Emporia State women were fairly well packed together with Stueve in 46th followed by Perez in 63rd, Lansing in 64th and Fisher in 69th place with less than a minute between them.

The women finished 10th of 11 teams in the MIAA with Schoenfeld leading the way in 17th, running a time of 23:03 for 6K. The Lady Hornets again did not enter a complete team at the Central Region Cross Country Championships held at Wayne State, Nebraska. Schoenfeld was the top finisher with a 52nd place finish in 23:29 for 6K.

2015

The ESU women opened the 2015 season with a dual against Newman. Emily Schoenfeld ran 19.23 over the 5K course to finish 2nd individually, but it wasn't enough, as Newman won the dual 19-42. The following weekend, the women competed at the Woody Greeno/Husker Invitational in Lincoln, Nebraska. Schoenfeld finished in the top 10 of the college division in 9th and was 33rd overall for the Hornet women. The Hornet women were without two of their top runners due to illness and finished 13th out of 14 teams in the college division.

ESU hosted their only home cross country meet of the year in Jones Park in Emporia. Schoenfeld continued to lead the Emporia State women by placing 5th individually in 18:49. The gap was 24 places back to the 29th place finish of Mallory Kramer, which led to the 5th place team finish for the Lady Hornets.

The Emporia State cross country teams competed on the same course that would be used for the 2015 MIAA Championships when they competed at the Fort Hays State Tiger Open at the Sand Plum Nature Trail in Victoria. Schoenfeld was the top finisher for the Emporia State women, placing 28th on the 5-kilometer course, as the women finished 13th. Two weeks after the Tiger Open, the Lady Hornets were back on the Fort Hays course for the MIAA Championships. Schoenfeld led the Hornets as she had all year by finishing 18th with a 23:03 over the 6K course. ESU finished a distant 10th out of 11 teams. Schoenfeld was the lone representative at the NCAA DII Regional held in Joplin, Missouri and placed 37th.

Epilogue

The Emporia State Women's Cross Country team began in 1980, the same year that the NAIA added women's cross country. As a pioneer in the establishment of women's cross country, the ESU teams met with outstanding success in the early years. During the 12 year history of Emporia State's participation in NAIA women's cross country, ESU established itself as one of the top teams in the nation. ESU posted national runner-up finishes twice, in 1980 and 1986, and five national top-ten finishes as well as eight top-20 finishes. Emporia State has had several successful runners at the NCAA DII and MIAA competitions. Eight athletes have earned All-American honors in their history.

The Hornets have competed in both NCAA and NAIA national competitions and in multiple different conferences in their 36 years of competition. Compared to their male counterparts the women's cross country history is much shorter in terms of years but has established their own legendary tradition.

Hornet History

ESU National Championship Teams

1958 Men's Cross Country NAIA   1962 Men's Cross Country NAIA
1959 Men's Cross Country NAIA   1963 Men's Cross Country NCAA
1961 Men's Cross Country NAIA

Men's Cross Country All-Americans

Year	Athlete	Meet	Place
1954	Bill Tidwell	NCAA	6th
1955	Bill Tidwell	NCAA	10th
1956	Bill Tidwell	NAIA	2nd
	Artie Dunn	NAIA	9th
1958	Paul Whiteley	NAIA	3rd
	Dennis Matheson	NAIA	4th
	Warner Wirta	NAIA	11th
1959	Paul Whiteley	NAIA	2nd
	Warner Wirta	NAIA	5th
	Dennis Matheson	NAIA	11th
1960	Dennis Matheson	NAIA	12th
1961	Richard Woelk	NAIA	6th
	John Camien	NAIA	12th
1962	**Ireland Sloan**	**NAIA**	**1st**
	John Camien	NAIA	3rd
	Richard Woelk	NAIA	7th
	Clarence Herpich	NAIA	13th
1963	**John Camien**	**NAIA**	**1st**
		NCAA	2nd
	Ireland Sloan	NAIA	2nd
	Richard Woelk	NAIA	12th
1964	**John Camien**	**NAIA**	**1st**
1968	Dennis Delmott	NAIA	12th
	David Brinsko	NAIA	15th
1969	Dennis Delmott	NAIA	9th
1971	Dennis Nee	NAIA	7th
1975	Greg Purkeypile	NAIA	25th
1976	Greg Purkeypile	NAIA	25th
1989	David Kipelio	NAIA	21st
1991	Gary Lyles	NAIA	16th
1993	Jermaine Mitchell	NCAA	15th
	Andrew LaRouche	NCAA	20th
1994	Jermaine Mitchell	NCAA	3rd
1996	Jermaine Mitchell	NCAA	7th

Women's Cross Country All-Americans

Year	Athlete	Meet	Place
1980	Lesha Wood	NAIA	4th
1981	Lesha Wood	NAIA	8th
1984	Kelly McCammon	NAIA	16th
1986	Susan Stine	NAIA	14th
	Amy Potter	NAIA	16th
1987	Cindy Blakely	NAIA	9th
1990	Jennifer Mullen	NAIA	20th
2002	Kadri Kelve	NCAA	13th
2006	Jonel Rossbach	NCAA	17th
2007	Jonel Rossbach	NCAA	4th

- **Bold=National Champion**

Men's All-Time Cross Country Participants

The listing of names is as complete and accurate as could be obtained from the sources used. There is a possibility that some who participated in cross country are not in this list.

Last	First	Yr 1	Yr 2	Yr 3	Yr 4	Yr 5
Akins	Robert	1981	1882	1983		
Allen	Todd	1989	1990	1992		
Andereck	Zack	2001				
Anderson	Brad	1971	1972	1973		
Anthony	Monroe	1999	2000			
Applegate	Mark	1978				
Applegate	Nolan	2001	2002	2003		
Applegate	Tyler	2001	2002	2003	2004	
Atkins	Charles	1960	1961	1962	1963	
Auerbach	Neil	1957				
Avery	Micheal	1978	1979	1980	1981	
Baker	Don	1964				
Ballou	Dan	1981	1982			
Barber	John	1960				
Barnett	Kevin	1997				
Barone	Roy	1969				
Bartels	Joe	1961				
Bartz	Tim	1989	1990	1991	1992	
Baumann	Bob	1959				
Baumgartel	Eric	1985				
Baxter	Josh	1992	1993	1995		
Beck	Nick	1999	2000			
Beckman	Robert	1977				
Beeman	Jon	1982	1983			
Bell	Chris	2000				
Bennett	Greg	1974				
Bennington	Sean	1993	1994			
Benson	Bill	1959				
Berry	Eric	1977				
Bird	Andrew	2000	2001	2002	2003	
Bisop	Rick	1970	1971	1972	1973	
Bliss	Richard	1956	1957			
Blow	Don	1954	1955	1956		
Bond	Ryan	2010				
Borgendale	Kevin	1974	1975			
Bosley	Cole	2015				
Bousom	Dave	1976				
Bowlin	James	2014	2015			
Boyle	Rick	1987	1989	1990		
Brading	Rick	1976	1977	1978		
Brammer	Scott	2001	2002	2003		
Brandley	Delbert	1971	1972	1973		
Brecheisen	Chad	1992	1993			
Brewer	Shawn	1987	1988	1989	1990	
Briggeman	Garth	1993	1994	1995	1996	1997
Brinsko	David	1965	1967	1968	1969	
Brokaw	Trey	2009	2010	2011		
Brough	Paul	1977				
Brown	Drake					
Brown	George	1954				
Brown	Ron	1966	1970			
Browne	John	1971	1972	1973	1974	
Browne	Tyrone	1967				
Brundage	Kurt	1998				
Bruning	Roger	1966	1967	1968	1969	
Bull	Jacob	2010	2011	2012	2013	
Burger	Greg	1985	1986			
Burgess	Denny	1954				
Burk	Mike	1974				
Burkdoll	Clint	1988				
Burns	Cody	2007	2008			
Burrows	John	1976	1977			
Byrne	Kevin	1977	1978	1979	1980	
Camien	John	1961	1962	1963	1964	
Camien	Robert	1964	1965	1966	1967	
Camien	Shea	2006				
Camien	Tom	1981				
Campell	Jonathon	1990	2000	2001		
Cantril	David	1979				
Carey	William	2014				
Cargill	Dennis	1985	1987			
Carlson	Brandon	1999	2000	2001	2002	
Carpenter	Greg	1968				
Carr	Tom	1946				
Carter	Tim	1964				
Caselman	Wade	1987	1988	1989	1990	
Certain	William	1960				
Cheatham	Heath	1985				
Christenson	Bryan	1981				
Claar	Eric	1993				
Clark	Peter	1959	1960	1961	1962	
Classen	Daniel	2012	2013	2014	2015	
Clifford	DePass	1965	1966	1967	1968	
Clults	Ronald	1964				
Clum	Steve	1989				
Clyma	David	1987				
Cohen	Edward	1959	1960			
Cole	Corey	1995	1996	1997	1998	
Combes	Justin	1984				
Cook	Jimmie	1972	1973			
Cool	Kirk	1984				
Cooley	Tye	1995	1996	1997	1998	
Cooper	Spence	1989				
Counts	Stephen	1958				
Cowling	Dillon	2008	2009	2010		
Cox	Richard	1983	1984			
Crabtree	Tom	1986	1987			

Craighead	John	1983			
Crotts	Larry	1958			
Cruz	Nick	1976	1977	1978	1979
Dain	Todd	1990	1991	1992	
Daniel	Jerry	1984	1985		
Davis	Bill	1954	1955		
Davis	Jack	1946			
Davis	Russel	1993			
Davis	Willard	1985			
Delmott	Asher	2008	2009	2010	2011
Delmott	Dennis	1966	1967	1968	1969
Delmott	Skyler	2006	2007	2008	2009
Denton	Chris	1995			
Dickerson	Kevin	1980	1981	1982	1983
Dilks	David	1980	1986		
Dittmer	Jared	2001			
Dolan	Jason	2000	2001	2003	
Downey	James	1956	1959		
Downs	George	1981			
Doyle	Tim	1966			
Dunn	Artie	1957			
Dunn	Eddie	1946			
Durbin	William	1967	1968		
Durkin	John	1967	1968		
Dvorak	Chris	2007	2008	2009	2010
Edmonds	Roger	2000	2001		
Edwards	Al	1960			
Eldridge	Aubrey	1955			
Enneking	Brian	1983			
Erbert	Collin	2011	2012		
Escher	Doug	1962			
Evely	John	1960	1961		
Farleigh	Sam	2003	2004		
Feldkamp	Mark	1985	1986		
Fick	Byron	1986	1987		
Finger	Robert	1962	1963	1964	1965
Fischer	Darin	1987			
Foraker	Pat	1995			
Foster	Chad	1997			
Foster	Larry	1959			
Frank	Garrett	2003			
Franklin	Landis	1957			
Franklin	Tom	1966	1967		
French	David	1960			
Fritz	Martin	1975			
Fulgham	J.M.	1960			
Gangel	Francis	1954	1955	1956	1957
Gehrke	David	1985			
George	David	1962	1963	1964	
George	David	1976	1977	1978	
Gibbs	George	1954	1955		
Gibson	David	2006			
Goentzel	Quentin	1965			
Goff	Grady	2010	2011		
Goulden	Clyde	1954			
Grady	Tom	1988	1989	1990	1991
Graham	Kale	2003			
Grank	Garett	2004			
Grant	Fisher	1979			
Gratto	Chuck	1976	1977	1978	
Grecian	Larry	1974	1975		
Grella	John	1964	1965		
Gruen	Ethan	1991			
Haag	Jason	1992			
Hahn	Ryan	2007	2008	2009	2010
Hall	Leonard	1973	1974	1975	1976
Hammond	James	1959			
Harber	Robert	1976	1977	1978	1979
Hardy	James	1986	1987		
Harlan	Mervin	1970			
Harrington	James	1963			
Harris	John-David	1998	1999	2000	2001
Havens	Tom	1977			
Hawkins	Steven	1979	1980	1981	1982
Hedges	Cale	2013			
Heffern	Bob	1963			
Heimer	Travis	1993	1994		
Hendrickson	Garland	1973			
Hendrin	Dennis	1965			
Hendry	Jason	1993	1994	1995	
Henicke	Jonathon	2006			
Henry	Cobb	1946			
Hensley	Frank	1966			
Herbert	Wade	1986			
Herpich	Clarence	1961	1962	1963	1964
Hertig	Matt	1989	1990		
Hickey	James	1972	1973		
Hicks	FRank	1958	1959		
Hicks	Roy	1955			
Hill	Will	2001	2002		
Hinton	Bob	1961			
Hinton		1965			
Hoffman	Peter	1976	1977	1978	1979
Hohmeier	William	2007	2008	2009	2010
Holland	Jason	1989	1990		
Holmes	Bret	1987			
Hornbaker	Andy	1974			
Housley	Robert	1955			
Hunt	Ron	1971			
Hutchinson	Clair	1954	1955		
Jackson	Jim	1946			
Jacobs	Bill	1966	1967		
James	Norman	1987			
James	Preston	1985			
Javier	Gonzalo	1956	1957	1958	1959
Jennings	Doug	1979	1980		
Jennings	Roger	1985	1986	1987	1988
Jilka	Adam	2001			

Johnson	Aidan	2015			
Jones	Lawrence	1955	1956		
Kaberline	Ryan	1993	1995		
Kariuki	Antoni	2002			
Karnes	Bob	1946			
Katzer	Josh	1998	1999		
Keach	David	2012			
Kennedy	Aaron	2001			
Kennedy	Jared	2001	2002	2003	
Kent	Johnny	1999			
Kern	Sloane	2007	2008		
Kerr	Dereck	2000			
Kidd	Mike	1996	1997	1998	
Kipelio	David	1989			
Knoll	Grant	2015			
Kodack	Mark	1968	1972		
Koppenhaver	Chris	1992	1994		
Kotzman	Kyle	2007	2008		
Kuestersteffan	Matt	1993			
Lacer	Josh	2010			
Laird	Richard	1970	1971		
Lane	Kenny	1987			
Lange	Erik	1996			
LaRouche	Andrew	1991	1992	1993	1994
LaRoche	Thomas	2014	2015		
Lawrence	John	1983			
Layne	Caleb	2015			
Leakey	Richard	1985			
Leis	John	1956			
Lewis	Sylvester	1961			
Limon	Lester	1965			
Linder	Robert	1954	1955		
Lonard	Bob	1960	1961		
Lopez	Henry	1967			
Love	Carl	1946			
Lovenstein	Rick	1982			
Lyles	Gary	1991			
Marquardt	Randy	1982	1983		
Martone	Tony	1955	1956		
Matheson	Dennis	1957	1958	1959	1960
Mathews	Chris	1978			
Mattox	Mike	1976	1977	1978	
Mayberry	Donald	1956			
McAllister	John	2000			
McCann	James	1962	1963		
McCleary	Josh	1994	1995	1996	1997	1998
McGovern	Adam	2007	2008	2009	2010
McKee		1965			
McPhee	James	1975	1976	1977	1978
McRoberts	Anthony	1972			
Meadows	Michael	2015			
Meyer	Eric	1998	1999	2000	
Mick	Richard	1991			
Miller	Cody	2010	2011	2013	2014
Miller	Gerald	1954			
Milliken	Arthur	1971	1972	1973	1974
Mills	Joe	1955	1956		
Mitchell	Jermaine	1993	1994	1995	1996
Mitchell		1965			
Mohr	Rodney	1969	1970	1971	
Moore	Charles	1946			
Moore	Harold	1946			
Moore	Justin	1992			
Moore	Wes	1983			
Morell	Jimmie	1967			
Mosier	Brian	2012	2013	2015	
Mosier	Mike	1981	1982		
Mosteller	Steve	1973	1974		
Nee	Dennis	1968	1969	1970	1971
Nevitt	Tom	1962	1963		
Newkirk	Adam	1998	1999	2000	2001
Newkirk	Brian	2015			
Nightengale	Brad	1979	1980		
Nofi	Joe	1964			
Nolte	Jason	1997			
Noonan	Tom	1976	1977	1978	1979
Norman	Jay C.	1959			
North	Eric	1977	1978		
Novacek	Joe	1994			
Oakley	Thomas	1981			
Obermier	Troy	1986			
Ochs	Mike	1959	1960		
Ohlde	David	1958	1959	1960	1961
O'Malley Jr.	Edward	1993			
Osterhaus	Shane	1998	199		
Palmer	Donnie	1992			
Panovich	Dean	1985			
Patterson	Darrell	1968	1969	1970	1971
Patton	Rick	1970	1971		
Pederson	Brian	1992			
Pense	Mike	1999			
Peterson	Steve	1984	1985	1986	
Pettit	Jason	1994	1995		
Piervincenzi	Bill	1960			
Pilkington	James	1957	1958		
Plank	Gary	1978	1979		
Ponder	David	1970			
Poole	George	1955	1956	1957	1958
Porter	Kirk	1982	1983	1984	
Portofee	Marcus	2010	2011	2012	
Prescia	Andy	1961			
Purkeypile	Greg	1973	1974	1975	1976
Quammen	Tom	1971			
Quillen	Daniel	2007	2008	2009	
Ramsey	Mark	1963			
Ransom	David	1975	1976	1977	1978
Rothlauf	David	1973	1974		
RedMond	Darrius	2011			

Last	First				
Reece	Bob	1971			
Reed	Lynn	1958	1959	1960	1961
Reed	Paul	1987	1988		
Reggie	DePass	1969			
Reynolds	Rob	1988			
Reynolds	Robert	1986			
Richard	Clasen	1960			
Riggs	Morgan	2010	2011	2012	2013	2014
Rinzler	Colton	2008			
Robben	Jason	1996	1997		
Roberts	DeWolff	1962	1963		
Rodina	Luke	2000	2001	2003	
Rodriguez	Iggy	1998	1999		
Rossheim	Barry	1975			
Rowley	Edward	1954			
Rowley	John	1978			
Salley	Shawn	2000			
Sams	Gabe	2015			
Schartz	Kenneth	1946			
Schenk	Jason	1986	1987		
Schierling	Valgene	1965			
Schmeidt	Robert	1967			
Schnurr	Jim	1967	1968		
Schrick	Raymond	1999	2000		
Sell	Steve	1966			
Seybold	John	1976	1977	1978	1979
Shaw	Paul	1965			
Sipe	Travis	2011	2015		
Skinner	Alex	2012	2013	2014	2015
Sloan	Ireland	1962	1963		
Smith	Brad	1997	1999		
Smith	Colby	1990	1991	1992	
Smith	Jordan	2011	2012	2013	2014	2015
Smith	Kent	1995			
Smith	Marrion	1997	1998	1999	
Smith	Will	2011			
Smitheran	Brent	1997	1998	1999	
Snyder	Derek	1978			
Stacy	Gale	1946			
Stacy	Ryan	2008			
Stamper	Woody	1991			
Stanbrough	Mark	1974	1975	1976	1977
Stander	Wayne	1956	1957	1959	
Staples	Kenan	1997			
Starks	Scott	1987	1988		
Starks	Scott	1988			
Staszkow	Myron	1963			
Stearnes	Chris	2004			
Steinbrink	Jonas	2002	2003		
Stephens	Michael	2004	2006	2007	
Sterner	Stever	1970	1971		
Stigge	Justin	1998	1999	2000	2002
Storck	Leon	1960	1961		
Sullivan	Colby	2001	2002	2003	
Summers	Marcus	2006	2007	2008	
Swaim	John	1963	1964	1965	1966
Swift	Jamin	1996	1997		
Syzmanski	Robert	1965	1966	1967	1968
Taylor	Aaron	2015			
Taylor	Rod	1986			
Tedrow	Rex	1970	1971		
Ternes	Brock	2004	2006	2007	
Ternes	Brock	2006	2007		
Terrell	Ray	1956			
Thomas	Blaine	1968	1969		
Thomas	Malcolm	1979			
Thomas	Shawn	1991	1992		
Thompson	Harold	1956	1957		
Thompson	Harry	1959	1960		
Thompson		1925	1926		
Tidwell	Billy	1954	1955	1956	
Tiffany	Scott	1987			
Tollefson	Troy	1986			
Tomlin	Chiffie	1961			
Topham	Greg	1978	1979		
Topham	Jeff	1971	1975	1976	
Torma	Thomas	1963	1964		
Travnichek	Vince	1983			
Trimlbe	Richard	1946			
Trites	Alan	1996	1997		
Tyler	Richard	1973	1974	1975	
Tyrrell	Steve	1989	1990	1991	
Van De Bruinhorst	Jack	1966	1967	1968	1969
Van Donge	Ted	1987			
Van Sickle	Ray	1970	1971	1972	1974
Velasquez	Ray	1954	1955	1956	1957
Voorhees	Warren	1985			
Waddell	Dwight	1946			
Wallace	Mike	1971	1972		
Wapelhorst	Kevin	1992			
Wayman	Andrew	2008	2009	2010	2011
Webb	Ed	1959			
Wecker	Brad	1988	1990	1991	
Wedeking	Tony	1971			
Weidenbach	Paul	1985	1986	1987	
Wellman	Eric	2003	2004	2006	2007
West	Bob	1956			
Weston	Charles	1973	1974	1975	1976
Weston	Ryan	2001	200	2003	2004
White	James	1962			
White	James	1970	1971		
Whiteley	Kenneth	1961	1962	1963	
Wienandt	Michael	2000			
Wiens	Luke	2000	2001	2002	2003
Wilson	Norman				
Woelk	Richard	1960	1961	1962	1963
Zimmerman	Paul	2010	2011	2012	2013

Women's All-Time Cross Country Participants

The listing of names is as complete and accurate as could be obtained from the sources used. There is a possibility that some who participated in cross country are not in this list.

Last	First	Yr 1	Yr 2	Yr 3	Yr 4	Yr 5	Last	First	Yr 1	Yr 2	Yr 3	Yr 4	Yr 5
Barnes	Abby	1994	1995	1996			Gray	Nancy	1980	1981	1982	1983	
Bates	Gloria	1985	1986				Graziano	Suzanne	1981	1982			
Baum	Tiffany	2007	2008	2009			Green	Ryan	2006				
Baum	Tiffany	2007					Griebel	Mary	1987				
Bennett	Robin	1989					Haight	Megan	2003	2004	2005		
Biggs	Lori	1994	1995				Hebb	Michelle	1989	1990	1991	1992	
Bina	Brenda	1990	1991	1992			Heber	Lisa	1988				
Blakely	Cindy	1987					Hein	Michelle	1999				
Bohm	Gretchen	1987	1988	1989			Herrick	Patty	1980	1981	1982		
Bookout	Kylie	2007	2008	2009			Hoffman	Kay	1980				
Brune	Kristin	1998					Hoover	Patty	1982				
Boswell	Jenna	2006					Hopkins	Cherie	1994	1995	1996		
Brune	Kristin	1997	1998	1999	2000	2001	Hudspeth	Tara	1997	1998	1999	2000	
Burr	Hannah	2009					Hurla	Missy	1988				
Carver	Cathy	1999	2000				Jagodzinske	Dana	1986				
Cathcart	Angela	1992	1993	1994	1995		Johnson	Adrienne	1996	1997	1998	1999	
Childers	Robin	1998	1999	2000			Jones	Brandy	2004				
Clanton	Chelsea	2007	2008				Julie	Hirt	1991				
Clem	Bridget	1995					Kantack	Tricia	2000				
Covington	Crystal	2001	2002	2003	2004		Kaschte	Suzy	1980				
Cuadra	Lindsay	2012	2013	2014			Kelley	Sharon	1989				
Daniel	Michele	1994	1995				Kelve	Kadri	2001	2002			
Davison	Kathryn	2007	2008	2009	2010		Kirkaldie	Lacy	1998	1999			
Diekmeier	Cori	2002					Kivitter	Carla	1986	1987	1988		
Dole	Holly	1994					Kolarik	Jean	1985		1986	1987	
Doubrava	Deandra	1997					Kramer	Mallory	2015				
Dryer	Stephanie	1985					Kronoshek	Suzie	1997				
Duran	Wendy	1997	1998	1999	2000		Lansing	Kayla	2012		2013		
Dutton	Jonelle	1983	1984	1986			Larimer	Shari	1984				
Edgerton	Cindy	1980	1981	1982			LaRouche	Amanda	1994				
Edwards	Laura	1992					Larson	Kristen	2002	2004	2005		
Feldkamp	Amy	2010	2011				Lee	Robyn	2005	2006			
Fennewald	Krysta	2004	2005	2006			Leverington	Megan	2002				
Ferguson	Sara	1998	1999	2000			Liddick	Kim	2001				
Fitzgerald	Maureen	1990					Lisa	Comstock	1991				
Folk	Aubrey	2006					Loyd	Kristin	2001	2003			
Fowler	Olivia	1993	1994				Lynn	Jamie	1992	1994			
Frazier	Ingrid	1990	1991				Lytle	Tiffany	2000	2001	2002		
Frehe	Morgan	2007	2008				Maddux	Courtney	2010				
Frey	Tara	1995	1996				Marshall	Stacy	2001				
Gant	Tetsey	2005					Martin	Amy	2011	2012			
Garhan	Susan	1981	1982	1983			Maureen	Fitzgerald	1991				
Garrison	Gabby	2012					May	Laura	1986	1987	1988	1989	
Gerber	Jalayne	1997					McCammon	Kelly	1981	1982	1983	1984	

McCumber	Lesa	2000			
Michelle	Bradbury	1991			
Mikesich	Darcy	1981	1982		
Mona	Katelyn	2008	2009	2010	2011
Moore	Amy	1993			
Moreland	Cicely	1989			
Mullen	Jennifer	1990	1991		
Murphy	Aileen	1997			
Murray	Tracey	1985			
Nilsson	Katarina	1994			
Oberg	Jessica	1995	1996		
Oltjen	Sydney	2010			
Orth	Tiffany	2011	2012		
Orton	Michelle	1982			
Page	Amy	1994	1995		
Pattison	Teresa	1985			
Pauly	Kayla	2001			
Peltz	Janine	2006			
Perez	Mercy	2014			
Phares	Cheryl	1980	1981		
Pitman	Kari	1995	1996	1997	1998
Posgai	Annette	1993	1994	1995	1996
Potter	Amy	1985	1986		
Proehl	Laura	1992			
Purcell	Charlotte	1984			
Ray	Jessica	1998			
Robison	Lacey	1996			
Ross	June	1986			
Ross	Billi	1994	1995		
Rossbach	Jonel	2004	2005	2006	2007
Schneider	Magali	1995	1996		
Schoenfeld	Emily	2013	2014		
Searcy	Trudy	1986			
Slack	Aniesa	2004	2005		
Smith	Jennifer	1992	1994	1994	
Smith	Sandra	1996	1997		
Staats	Dominique	2012			
Stine	Susan	1985	1986	1987	1989
Stine	Kerry	1990			
Stoll	Ann	1985			
Strader	Jennifer	1986	1987	1988	
Strickland	Kati	2012	2013	2014	
Stueve	Taylor	2012	2013	2014	
Swaney	Carol	1980	1981		
Teichgraeber	Peggy	1983	1984	1986	
Trunecek	Stacey	2003			
Turner	Nicole	2001			
Tyrrell	Michelle	1987	1988	1989	1990
VanDurme	Andria	1989			
Visser	Melissa	2003	2004		
Wallace	Carolyn	2011	2012	2013	2014
Walter	Sarah	1996	1997		
Weller	Christy	2008	2009		
Welte	Susan	2012	2013	2014	
Wheeler	Katie	1989	1990		
White	Jennifer	1998			
Willse	Jaci	2009			
Wilson	Casey	1997	1998	1999	
Wolf	Jennifer	1993	1994		
Wolford	Kathy	1987			
Wood	Lesha	1980	1981	1982	
Woods	Terri	1980			
Wymore	Dena	1982			
Yelliot	Kayci	2010			
Yingst	Janice	2000			
Young	Cassandra	1998			
Zeller	Amy	2002			

Resources

Athletic Department Track/Field and Cross Country Records and Releases. Emporia State University, Emporia, KS.

Bulletin (Emporia State University student newspaper). Emporia State University, Emporia, KS.

Crowther, S. & Ruhl, A. (1905). *Rowing and Track Athletics.* New York: MacMillan Co.

Emporia Gazette. Emporia, KS. Newspaper.

Ensminger, L.G. (1982). *A History of Men's Intercollegiate Athletics at Kansas State Teachers College, Emporia, 1942-1952, with implications of World War II.* Unpublished master's thesis, Kansas State Teachers College, Emporia, KS.

Markowitz (1962*). Football, for the Sport of it: A History of Football from 1893 to 1962 at the Kansas State Teachers College of Emporia.* Emporia, KS: Emporia State Press.

Official Records Book of the National Association of Intercollegiate Athletics. (1958-1983). (Published September yearly, beginning 1958). Kansas City, MO: NAIA.

Olympic Track and Field. (1979). Los Altos, CA: Track and Field News.

San Romani, Archie. (1960). (Speech delivered to the National Collegiate Track Coaches Association, title "New Horizons in High School Distance Running"). The Pan American Track and Field Journal, pp. 89-92.

State Normal Monthly. (1900, April). Vo. XII, No.7, p. 107. Emporia State University, Emporia, KS.

Student Index. (1902). Vol. 1, No. 17, p. 217. Emporia State University. Emporia, KS.

Sunflower. (1898-2015). (Annual Yearbook). Emporia State University. Emporia, KS.

Taylor, B. (1947). *History of Athletics at Kansas State Teachers College.* Emporia, KS. Unpublished master's thesis, Kansas State Teachers College, Emporia.

Watts, J. (1976). *A History of Women's Athletics at Emporia State, 1900-1976.* Unpublished manuscript, Emporia Kansas State College, Emporia.

Ziegler, Eearle M. (1979). *History of Physical Education and Sport. Englewood Cliffs.* NJ: Prentice-Hall Inc.

About the Author

Dr. Mark Stanbrough ran cross country and track and field for the Emporia State Hornets from 1974-1977 and was the head track and field and cross country coach at Emporia State from 1984-1992.

Dr. Stanbrough is a professor in the Department of Health, Physical Education and Recreation at Emporia State University in Kansas. He teaches graduate and undergraduate exercise physiology and sports psychology classes and is the director of Coaching Education. The Coaching Education program at Emporia State is currently one of only 10 universities in the United State to be accredited by the National Council for the Accreditation of Coaching Education. He was a co-founder of the online physical education graduate program, the first in United States to go completely online. He received his Ph.D. in exercise physiology from the University of Oregon, and undergraduate and master's degrees from Emporia State in physical education. He has served as department chair and has served on the National Association for Sport and Physical Education National Sport Steering Committee and is a past member of the board of directors for the National Council for the Accreditation of Coaching Education.

Mark has over 30 years of coaching experience at the collegiate, high school, middle school and club level. He has also coached at Emporia High School and Glasco High School in Kansas. He is a member of the Emporia State University Athletic Hall of Honor and the Health, Physical Education, Recreation Hall of Honor and has won numerous coach-of-the-year awards at the high school and collegiate levels.

After graduating from Silver Lake High School, Steve Hawkins competed in track and field/cross country at Emporia State University from 1979 to 1983. He served as a graduate assistant coach at ESU from 1983-1985. Steve is currently a Professor in the Exercise Science department at California Lutheran University in Thousand Oaks, California, and he also serves as chair of the department. He is a Fellow of the American College of Sports Medicine, and has served as President of the Southwest Regional Chapter of the ACSM. Steve has extensive teaching and research experience in the physiology of exercise, with particular emphasis on aging's influence, and he has published widely on master athletes, including chapters in two textbooks on aging and exercise. Steve has also taught at California State University, Los Angeles, and USC. Steve was inducted into the ESU Department of HPER Hall of Honor in 2009.